How t Read Daniel

Tremper Longman III

ivp
Academic
An imprint of InterVarsity Press
Downers Grove, Illinois

InterVarsity Press
P.O. Box 1400, Downers Grove, IL 60515-1426
ivpress.com
email@ivpress.com

InterVarsity Press® is the book-publishing division of InterVarsity Christian Fellowship/USA®, a movement of students and faculty active on campus at hundreds of universities, colleges, and schools of nursing in the United States of America, and a member movement of the International Fellowship of Evangelical Students. For information about local and regional activities, visit intervarsity.org.

All Scripture quotations, unless otherwise indicated, are taken from The Holy Bible, New International Version®, NIV®. Copyright © 1973, 1978, 1984, 2011 by Biblica, Inc.™ Used by permission of Zondervan. All rights reserved worldwide. www.zondervan.com. The "NIV" and "New International Version" are trademarks registered in the United States Patent and Trademark Office by Biblica, Inc.™

Cover design and image composite: David Fassett
Interior design: Jeanna Wiggins
Images: Daniel in the Lion's Den illustration © CatLane / DigitalVision Vectors / Getty Images

ISBN 978-0-8308-5320-5 (print)
ISBN 978-0-8308-5321-2 (digital)

Printed in the United States of America ♾

InterVarsity Press is committed to ecological stewardship and to the conservation of natural resources in all our operations. This book was printed using sustainably sourced paper.

Library of Congress Cataloging-in-Publication Data
A catalog record for this book is available from the Library of Congress.

P 23 22 21 20 19 18 17 16 15 14 13 12 11 10 9 8 7 6 5 4 3 2 1

Y 37 36 35 34 33 32 31 30 29 28 27 26 25 24 23 22 21 20

"Daniel is a fascinating but complicated book—historically, theologically, and critically. Longman has the wonderful ability to distill information and summarize academic debates in a highly readable style. He has accomplished that service with other books in the series, and now he gifts us with this volume. A helpful and thoroughly practical introduction."

M. Daniel Carroll R., Blanchard Professor of Old Testament, Wheaton College and Graduate School

"Tremper Longman's *How to Read Daniel* is a fantastic read! He leads his reader thoughtfully through hungry lions, fiery furnaces, and monstrous beasts to show how Daniel reminds us that God is not only present but in control, even in the darkest places. This book provides a stirring reminder that God has the ultimate victory. He can care for us, even in toxic environments, and he meets us in the midst of a troubled world as the ultimate victorious King."

Beth M. Stovell, associate professor of Old Testament at Ambrose University and national catalyst for theological and spiritual formation for Vineyard Canada

"Tremper Longman III provides the ideal companion for reading the book of Daniel. He helps us understand the relationship between the cheering stories of the first half and the weird visions of the second half, by showing how both were intended to encourage God's people in the midst of suffering and persecution. He helps us avoid simplistic messages from the stories and fanciful messages from the visions. Balanced, informative, and readable, this is a great tool for any preacher or Bible study leader."

Christopher J. H. Wright, Langham Partnership, author of *Hearing the Message of Daniel: Sustaining Faith in Today's World*

To my wife, Alice

Contents

Acknowledgments

I am pleased to present the sixth volume in the How to Read series. The first volume on the Psalms came out near the beginning of my writing career in 1987, and now over thirty years later comes *How to Read Daniel*.

What a privilege it is to be able to write these books that present the fruits of my scholarly explorations in what I intend (and hope) is an accessible form. I write these books for people who are not biblical scholars but for very intelligent lay people, pastors, and seminarians.

I would like to take this opportunity to thank my editors at InterVarsity Press over the years for encouraging me and guiding me in the writing of these books. Jim Hoover asked me to write *How to Read Psalms*, and Dan Reid provided excellent editorial guidance for this book and the next four (*Proverbs*, *Genesis*, *Exodus*, *Job* [with John Walton]). Before he retired, Dan asked me to write *How to Read Daniel* and then passed it off to his successor, Anna Gissing, who provided excellent editorial feedback.

I dedicate this book, as I have many of my books, to my lovely and intelligent wife, Alice. I love Alice, and she loves me, but even more importantly she loves God and his Word. She brings the best out of me and keeps me grounded in my relationship with God.

Tremper Longman III
November 2019

Introduction

Invitation to the Book of Daniel

The fiery furnace, the writing on the wall, the lion's den—these are among the most memorable moments in the first six chapters of the book of Daniel. Four monstrous beasts rising from a chaotic sea, one "like a son of man," "seventy sevens," kings of the North and kings from the South, the righteous rising "like the stars for ever and ever"—these are among the most striking descriptions of the second six chapters of the book of Daniel.

In the first six chapters, we read stirring stories of Daniel and the four friends' faith in the midst of a hostile and dangerous culture. In the second six chapters, we read about Daniel's disturbing, yet ultimately encouraging, visions of the future.

What are we to make of it all? What does it all mean, and does the book speak to us today? These are the questions that motivate the writing of this book, and as we answer them, we will see that the author of the book of Daniel not only spoke loud and clear to his generation but also to ours: in spite of present circumstances, God is in control, and he will have the final victory!

We will explore this fascinating but ancient book in three parts in order to come to grips with how to read it in the twenty-first century. In the first part, we will focus on overarching issues that influence our understanding of the message of the book to its original audience and set up how we should then appropriate it today. Part one deals with literary issues (genre, language, and structure, chap. 1), historical setting (both for the background of the book and the date of its final composition, chap. 2), and its main theological message (chap. 3).

In part two, we will take a closer look at the contents of the book with an emphasis on its meaning for the original audience. We start by examining the six stories of Daniel and his three friends in a foreign court found in Daniel 1–6. First we will look at the tales of court contest found in Daniel 1, 2, 4, and 5 (chaps. 4–7) and then at the tales of court conflict found in Daniel 3 and 6 (chaps. 8 and 9). After covering the stories of the first six chapters of Daniel, we move on to a close look at the four apocalyptic visions found in Daniel 7:1–12:4 (chaps. 10–13). Last, we will take a brief look at the final instructions given to Daniel (Dan 12:5-13) after all his experiences in the court and in the spiritual realm (chap. 14).

Finally, part three views the message of Daniel from the perspective of the twenty-first century. In particular, we explore how the first six chapters help us live a faithful life in the midst of a culture toxic or even hostile to our faith (chap. 15) and the latter six chapters provide us comfort and hope as we live in a difficult and often dangerous world (chap. 16).

PART 1

Reading Daniel in Its Original Setting

This book, like its predecessors in the How to Read series, is not a commentary. While it includes commentary (see especially part two), the purpose is to orient the reader to a proper reading of the book of Daniel. Thus, we are interested in questions of interpretive method and its application.

Accordingly, part one presents an overview of the book from a literary, historical, and theological perspective. In the three chapters that follow, we examine the genre, structure, style, and language of Daniel (chap. 1) as well as the historical background (chap. 2) and the major theological message of the book (chap. 3).

ONE

Stories and Visions in the Midst of Oppression

Genre, Language, and Structure

The book of Daniel has a most curious structure. The first six chapters tell six different, though related, stories. They present four noble Judean young men, Daniel and his three friends (Hananiah, Mishael, and Azariah), as political hostages in a foreign court. The six separate stories, one in each chapter, are each set in either the Babylonian (Dan 1–5) or Persian (Dan 6) courts. The four men are exiles, but they are also trained and take their place in the center of power. These stories, as we will see, conform to ancient Near Eastern protocol but also serve as models for the behavior of God's people when they find themselves in situations of oppression. We will unpack these matters in later chapters, but for now, notice how these six chapters contrast in style and format with the last six chapters (Dan 7–12).

The opening six stories in many ways are straightforward. We will see that these narratives have relatively simple plots and clearly delineated characters. While interesting and profound, they are not complicated when studied closely in their ancient context. On the contrary, the second half of the book contains symbolic visions that, particularly to a modern audience, are mind-boggling and extremely difficult to understand. Hybrid beasts arise out of a chaotic sea. One like a son of man rides a cloud into the presence of the Ancient of Days. A ram and a goat butt each other. An angel speaks about seventy weeks of years. The final vision presents the future in terms of alternating kings of the North and kings of the South.

Many modern readers find the type of literature found in the last six chapters of the book very difficult to understand beyond the idea that the four visions (Dan 7; 8; 9; 10–12) point to some disaster at the end. Christians who read Daniel 7–12 are reminded of the book of Revelation and often, like Revelation, find the message confusing as well as a bit frightening. Many choose to avoid the book.

Of course, if we avoid the book or misunderstand it, then we will miss a critical part of God's message to us. And we will see that the book—both parts—is not as difficult to understand as we might think at first glance, provided we read it on its own terms and in the context of its original culture.

GENRE

Court tales (Dan 1–6). We begin with an introduction to the genres of the book. All six stories of these chapters are set in a court foreign to Daniel and his three friends. We learn in the first chapter, which serves as a kind of introduction to the rest of the stories, that Daniel and his three friends were forcibly relocated to Babylon, an empire that had successfully compelled the nation of Judah to assume vassal status in its rapidly expanding empire. As is typical to such scenarios in the ancient Near East, the sovereign nation makes the vassal nation send some people from its noble class to the heart of the empire for training (really indoctrination) and redeployment to serve the interests of the empire. We will say more about these matters below, but this opening explains the reason for the setting of these six chapters. At first, Daniel and his three friends, among the noble class of Judah so deported, find themselves in the Babylonian court of Nebuchadnezzar down through the end of the Babylonian Empire. But then, when the Persians defeat the Babylonians (see chap. 2), they will serve in the Persian court.

We refer to these six chapters as tales, but we do not intend to communicate the idea that they are pure fiction. They are not fairy tales. Many scholars today reject their historical reliability, but many other scholars, myself included, would disagree. We will discuss the historical truthfulness of the book of Daniel later (chap. 2), but for now I simply want to explain that I refer to them as tales, not because I believe they are made-up stories but rather because they have a story-like character.

Hans Frei, a well-respected Yale theologian of a generation ago, famously spoke of the narratives of the Old Testament as "history-like stories."[1] I think he got this exactly reversed, though his quote indicates that he rightly saw that there was a historical character to these narratives that also displayed a literary brilliance. I would capture the same reality by saying that much of the narrative in the Old Testament, including Daniel 1–6, is "story-like history." And so I think it is fair to use the term "tale" in respect to Daniel 1–6 as long as we realize that such a term does not undermine the historical referentiality of these chapters.

But what kind of tales are they?

Because of their setting, scholarship appropriately calls them "court tales." But they can be divided into two primary types: tales of "court contest" and tales of "court conflict."[2]

A tale of court contest describes a scene in which a superior has a problem that needs to be solved, and he enlists his subordinates to help him resolve the problem, and then the subordinates engage in a type of competition to do so. The party that resolves the issue then receives an appropriate reward. This general plot summary describes Daniel 1, 2, 4, and 5, though we will wait till later chapters to describe how their specific plots fit into this general pattern. We will see how this type of tale highlights the vast superiority of the God of Daniel and his three friends over the false gods of the Babylonians.

The two tales of court conflict that we have in Daniel 3 and 6 achieve the same goal of promoting Yahweh over the false gods of the Babylonians. These chapters display the animosity that the Babylonian wise men had toward the Hebrew youths. By chapter 3, the latter have been promoted due to their success in the court contests (thanks to God). Now envy sets in as their Babylonian peers do their best to sabotage their careers and even their lives. Again, we will describe the specific plots when we come to later chapters, but we will see how God intervenes to preserve the lives and promote the careers of the three friends (Dan 3) and Daniel (Dan 6).

Apocalyptic visions (Dan 7–12). While the first six chapters are court tales, the last six are four visions that are rightly described as apocalyptic. The English term *apocalyptic* derives from a Greek term (*apokalypsis*) that appears in the opening verse of the book of Revelation ("the apocalypse of Jesus Christ"). Indeed, the word in Greek is often translated "revelation" and ends up giving the book its name in the English tradition. In many ways, to be discussed later, the book of Daniel is similar (of the same genre) as the book of Revelation, and both can be described as apocalyptic books. But what are the characteristics of apocalyptic literature?

As we mentioned, the Greek term *apokalypsis* means "revelation," and we begin there. Apocalyptic is a form of divine revelation given to human beings. But, of course, there is more than one type of revelation in the Bible. The term *apocalyptic* describes the type of revelation that is found in Daniel and Revelation and some portions of the Old Testament that have some or all of the same characteristics as those two books (Is 24–27; parts of Zechariah) as well as a number of extrabiblical books written in the intertestamental period through the time of the New Testament (1 Enoch, 4 Ezra, and 2 Baruch, for example). What these biblical and extrabiblical books have in common will be described in the following paragraphs.

The revelation of the future that we refer to as *apocalyptic* has certain features that we might compare and contrast to what might be called *classical prophecy*, which also contains revelation about the future. While the Bible has many examples of the latter (for instance, Isaiah, Jeremiah, Ezekiel, and the twelve Minor Prophets), we will illustrate this comparison and contrast it by looking at the differences between Daniel and Jeremiah.

First, we should note that the revelations that God gives Daniel and Jeremiah have different goals, and this difference leads to different tasks for the two men.

God gives Jeremiah a vision of the future in order to encourage the people to whom he is speaking to repent and avoid that future. Jeremiah speaks to the people in his community to tell them that they have sinned by breaking the covenant with God through their idolatry and other behaviors, and so they will be punished according to the curses of the covenant. Among the curses are those that warned about defeat at the hand of an enemy and exile from the land (see, for example, Deut 28:25-29).

Thus, prophets like Jeremiah can be called *covenant lawyers*. God uses them to accuse the people of violations of the law and to threaten them with punishments drawn from the curses of the covenant unless they repent (see Deut 27 and 28). For this reason, Jeremiah receives God's revelation, which he shares with the people in the hope that they repent. As it turns out, they don't repent, and so eventually God tells Jeremiah to change his tune and just announce the coming judgment. The point is that a prophet shares the revelation with the people.

When we turn to Daniel in the apocalyptic portion of the book, the first thing we notice is that God never speaks to Daniel directly. Instead, Daniel has visions or dreams that disturb him. Eventually, an angelic interpreter (when given a name, Gabriel) comes and explains the vision or dream to him. Then, surprisingly at first, we notice that Daniel is never charged to share his revelation with the people. Indeed, at one point he is told to "roll up and seal the words of the scroll until the time of the end" (Dan 12:4).

These differences between Jeremiah and Daniel may be found in the purpose of the revelation given to them. Daniel does not speak to God's people with the hope of leading them to repent. Daniel's visions have the purpose of reassuring the people in the midst of their oppression and persecution that God has control of the situation and will ultimately bring judgment on their oppressors.

Thus, while prophets are often the bearers of bad news for the people of God ("you have sinned, and you will be punished unless you repent"), Daniel is the bearer of good news ("though you are living under oppression, know that God is in control and will have the final victory"). The book of Revelation, the other major example of apocalyptic literature in the Bible, has the same dynamic as the book of Daniel.

But there are other features of content and style that differentiate revelation of the future given to prophets like Jeremiah from revelation of the future given to Daniel.

The first has to do with the far-reaching nature of their respective interest in the future. Since prophets are interested in an immediate response of repentance, they typically speak about relatively near-term possibilities. While this does not mean that some of their oracles do not have longer-term ramifications, they usually speak of things that will happen near-term.

For instance, many modern readers of Isaiah 7:14 ("Therefore the Lord himself will give you a sign: The virgin will conceive and give birth to a son, and will call him Immanuel") will see that it has a clear near-term fulfillment. After all, in context Isaiah is speaking to King Ahaz, who is worried about a threat from two kings, Pekah of the Northern Kingdom and Rezin of Aram (Syria). Isaiah is telling him that he should not worry and either cave to their demands or ally himself with Assyria, which he eventually does because God will take care of him. The birth of the child to the virgin (or "young woman") is a sign that will indicate to Ahaz that God is indeed speaking through Isaiah. Therefore, it is something that will happen relatively soon since by the time this son "will be eating curds and honey when he knows enough to reject the wrong and choose the right, . . . the land of the two kings you dread will be laid waste" (Is 7:15-16). The text couldn't be more obvious that even this famous verse, while having an intensified fulfillment in the birth of Jesus, found its original fulfillment in the years right after it was uttered.

On the other hand, apocalyptic literature, such as Daniel and Revelation, has its ultimate sights not on the near-term future but on the far-distant future, indeed the end of time. After all, the focus is on God's ultimate and everlasting victory. This does not mean that Daniel and Revelation don't speak about present realities or even more short-term future realities, but these are in the service of talking about God's great victory at the end.

We can see another difference, at least in degree, in the type of language we find in apocalyptic and prophetic literature. Apocalyptic literature describes the future in highly figurative language. Now, don't get me wrong; vivid imagery fills the pages of Scripture. Genesis depicts the creation of the first human being as a result of God (who is a spirit) forming him from dust and breathing into his nostrils. Samson snaps the bowstrings with which Delilah bound him "as easily as a piece of string snaps when it comes close to a flame" (Judg 16:9). The poetic portions of the Old Testament bombard the reader with metaphors and similes. In the book of Psalms, God is described as a king (Ps 47), a shepherd (Ps 23), a warrior (Ps 7), a mother of a weaned child (Ps 131), a drunk soldier (Ps 78:65), and on and on. Prophets like Jeremiah use imagery as well to communicate their message. In an oracle in Jeremiah 24, God describes his people to Jeremiah as two baskets of figs. The good figs are the exiles, but the bad figs are people like King Zedekiah, his officials and those who are still living in the land of Judah, and those who escaped to Egypt.

While virtually every chapter of the Old Testament contains figurative language of one sort or another, apocalyptic literature (Daniel, Revelation, and extrabiblical apocalyptic sources) has a certain distinctive and strikingly pervasive use of figurative language. Daniel 7 speaks of monstrous beasts rising out of a turbulent sea. Daniel 8 pictures two warring nations as a goat with a large horn butting a ram that had two horns. Daniel 9 turns the seventy years of the exile announced by Jeremiah into "seventy 'sevens,'" in what is one of many examples of the figurative use of numbers in Daniel and in apocalyptic literature generally. Daniel 10 describes a celestial figure "dressed in linen, with a belt of fine gold from Uphaz around his waist. His body was like topaz, his face like lightning, his eyes like flaming torches, his arms and legs like the gleam of burnished bronze, and his voice like the sound of a multitude" (Dan 10:5-6). Daniel 12 describes the "wise," who we will later see are the likely audience of the book of Daniel, as those who will "shine like the brightness of the heavens, and those who lead many to righteousness, like the stars for ever and ever" (Dan 12:3).

The imagery strikes modern readers as bizarre and obscure. We will explore the meaning of these and the other images later in this book, but for now we should note that the characteristic imagery of apocalyptic literature, while odd to us, was not odd to its ancient, original audience. We will see that much of it draws on well-known ancient Near Eastern mythology (the sea and its beasts representing chaos and evil) and previous biblical ideas (hybrid beasts as unclean and therefore repulsive). Many modern readers encounter these images and shake their heads, whereas an ancient audience would have instinctively known the significance of this language. Again, this reminds us how important it is to put ourselves in the place of the ancient reader as we interpret the books of the Old Testament.

Further, apocalyptic literature paints the world past, present, and future in highly contrastive terms. Scholars often speak of apocalyptic literature's perspective as dualistic in terms of time, place, and ethics. The author thinks in terms of the present and the future, the earth and heaven, and evil and good. There are no gray areas. He describes the present earthly reality as evil as he gives hope that the future heavenly existence will be good.

Finally, it is not hard to find those who describe apocalyptic literature as pessimistic. After all, the present is evil and the people of God are experiencing oppression and persecution. And the future is going to bring judgment and devastation. It all sounds very depressing.

But then such an evaluation depends on what side of the divide one is on. For the oppressor, the news is bad. For the persecuted, the news is good. As we will see throughout this book, Daniel has one overriding message that he is communicating to God's faithful, oppressed people (the "wise," Dan 12:3): in spite of present circumstances, God is in control. He will have the final victory. I submit that, rather than being pessimistic, apocalyptic literature is optimistic. God's people will be freed from their oppression, while those who harm them will be punished.

LANGUAGE AND STRUCTURE

We have already observed how the book of Daniel can be divided into two big parts: the first six chapters are six separate court tales, and the second six chapters are four apocalyptic visions. Such a division of the book seems like a neat division in to two discrete and separate parts, but there are features that bind these two parts together.

I have also already mentioned what is the most important feature that binds these two parts together—the central theme. Each of the six tales and four visions seek to assure the reader that God is in control and will have the final victory. I will explain how these tales and visions propel this message when we come to part two of the present book.

The second feature that connects these two parts of the book are the languages in which the chapters were written. Yes, that's right, languages. Almost all of the rest of the Old Testament, with the exception of a large part of the book of Ezra (4:8–6:18; 7:12-26) was written in Hebrew, but about half of Daniel was written in Aramaic. We might expect that the language divide would mirror the genre divide, but it doesn't—at least not perfectly.

The book opens in Hebrew and continues in that language until we come to Daniel 2:4, where the narrator tells us that in response to a demand by King Nebuchadnezzar, "the astrologers answered the king in Aramaic," and then the language shifts from Hebrew to Aramaic.[3]

The fact that the Babylonian astrologers would speak in Aramaic is not particularly surprising since that was the everyday language of the Babylonian court. By that time, Aramaic was also the lingua franca (international language of diplomacy, finance, and politics) of the day, so the Hebrew reader would be able to read it. By shifting to Aramaic, the text gains vividness and realism.

What is surprising, though, is that the language of the text does not shift back to Hebrew after the Babylonian astrologers speak. Indeed, the book of Daniel continues to be written in Aramaic until the end of chapter 7. And then it shifts back to Hebrew from chapter 8 until the end of the book in chapter 12.

Various theories have been given for why this language shift happens, but none of these theories have gotten much traction among a broader group of scholars. Fortunately, not knowing why does not affect our ability to read the book with understanding. The only reason why I am even bringing it up, besides the fact that it is an interesting fact, is that we should notice how the language change does not conform to the genre change, binding the two parts together.

And this observation leads to another one that further solidifies the connection between the two parts (court tales and apocalyptic visions) and also offers a further insight into the structure of the book. The Aramaic portion of the book (chaps. 2–7) incorporates five of the court tales and the first apocalyptic vision, which relate to each other by means of a characteristically Hebrew way called *chiasm*.

Chiasm, as a structuring device, derives its name from the Greek letter chi, which is an X. Thus, the name indicates a structure that has a crossing pattern. This crossing pattern can be of different lengths and complexity but typically highlights similarity between the first and last unit, then the second and second-to-last unit, the third and third-to-last unit, and potentially further.

```
A
   B
      C
         D
         D'
      C'
   B'
A'
```
Figure 1.1

While this pattern occurs in Hebrew literature from the verse level to the book level, some biblical readers see chiasms all over the place when they are not there. That admitted, Daniel 2 through 7 does appear to be in a chiastic relationship.

The similarity between the paired chapters extends to the details of the plots or the similarity of the related dream and vision. The structure firmly connects the two parts of Daniel (tales and visions), so they should be read together even if they had different origins. It also highlights the introductory role of the first chapter.

Daniel 1 connects to Daniel 8–12 by its language (Hebrew) but clearly serves as an introduction to the entire book. As we will see, the chapter introduces the main protagonists (Daniel and his three friends) and explains how they came to Babylon. The plot of the chapter informs

A: A Dream of a Statue Representing Four Kingdoms (Daniel 2)

    B: A Court Conflict: The Three Friends in the Fiery Furnace (Daniel 3)

        C: A Court Contest: Interpreting Nebuchadnezzar's Dream (Daniel 4)

        C': A Court Contest: Interpreting the Writing on the Wall (Daniel 5)

    B': A Court Conflict: Daniel in the Lions' Den (Daniel 6)

A': A Vision of Beasts Representing Four Kingdoms (Daniel 7)

Figure 1.2

us about the deep faith of the four men who are living in a culture that is toxic to their faith. Thus, the chapter sets the reader up for the following court tales and provides the setting for the four visions. That said, we will see that it does have a close connection with Daniel 2 because it continues the story of how the successes of the four are not the result of their Babylonian training but the result of God's grace (see chap. 5).

SUMMARY

The book of Daniel contains six stories about Daniel in a foreign court (chaps. 1–6) and four apocalyptic visions (chaps. 7–12). In later chapters, we will dig into the contents of these stories and visions and see that, though there are interesting differences between them, they all have the same basic theme or message: in spite of present difficulties, God is in control, and he will have the final victory. In this chapter, we dug down into the nature of the six stories as composed of tales of court contest and tales of court conflict. We also explored the nature of the apocalyptic visions, particularly as they differed from prophetic revelation. We noticed, too, that the book of Daniel, like Ezra, was written in two languages (Hebrew and Aramaic) so that the languages linked the two halves of the book. This linkage between the two halves was also observed in the chiasm that is formed in chapters 2 through 7.

DISCUSSION QUESTIONS

1. What makes the first six chapters of Daniel different than the last six?

2. What links the two halves of the book (Dan 1–6 and 7–12) together?

3. What is a chiasm, and where do you find a chiasm?

4. Where do you find a chiasm in the book of Daniel? What function does it serve in the book?

TWO

Babylonian Exile and Persian (and Greek) Domination

The Historical Setting of the Book of Daniel

The Bible was not written to us. That statement may sound shocking at first, so let me quickly say that while the Bible was not written *to* us, it was certainly written *for* us. But Bible readers in the twenty-first-century AD need to understand and take into account that the book was written in antiquity and in a particular culture (Israelite) to a contemporary audience who had their own particular questions and concerns. In order to rightly apply the book to our lives, we have to know something about the time period in which it was written and the people for whom it was written.

We need to know both the historical context that lies behind the book and the particular historical context of the first audience. As we will see, the first topic is uncontroversial but important, while the second is very controversial but less important for understanding the effect of the book.

DANIEL'S TIME AND PLACE IN HISTORY

We will first look at the historical background presented by the book itself for the six court tales and the four apocalyptic visions. The plot of the book begins squarely in the Neo-Babylonian period and extends through the early Persian period.

The book begins: "In the third year of the reign of Jehoiakim king of Judah, Nebuchadnezzar king of Babylon came to Jerusalem and besieged it" (Dan 1:1). The third year of Jehoiakim would be sometime around 606/605 BC. All the first readers of the book of Daniel would know the backstory. Readers today know the story from the biblical histories as well as from ancient Near Eastern sources that have been discovered over the past century and a half from archaeological sites in the area that was ancient Babylon (modern-day Iraq, particularly the southern part).

The last chronological reference in the book while Daniel is still alive is found in the first verse of Daniel 10: "In the third year of Cyrus king of Persia." The third year of Cyrus was approximately 536 BC. Thus the events of the life of Daniel covered by the book extends from 606/605 BC to 536 BC. We will take a closer look at what we know about this time period below. But before we do, let's review the history that leads up to this moment in time.

THE DEEP BACKGROUND TO THE STORY OF DANIEL

The Bible contains one grand narrative of God's care for his human creatures. We come to a richer understanding of any portion of that narrative by understanding its place in the whole. Thus, we begin our study of the background of the book of Daniel by giving a brief reminder of where we are in the biblical narrative when we start the book of Daniel.

To root Daniel's story in the deep past of the Bible, we begin with the account of creation. According to Genesis 1–2, God created everything, including human beings.[1] At that time humans were given the status of divine image bearers; they were innocent and capable of moral choice. Genesis 3 tells the story of how humans used their moral choice to assert their own independence rather than to follow the guidance of God. Thus, as Paul later says, for the first time sin and death became a part of human experience (Rom 5:12-21).

God judges the sin of Adam and Eve. But he still extends his grace to them (symbolized by him giving them clothing). Their sin led to alienation from God, so they no longer lived in his presence but had to build special holy places (altars) and offer sacrifices to draw close to him.[2] That sin separated humans from their holy God is not surprising. What is amazing is that God does not give up on his human creatures but rather pursues reconciliation with them.

Genesis 3–11 presents four stories: Adam and Eve's rebellion (Gen 3), Cain killing Abel (Gen 4:1-16), the flood (Gen 6–9), and the Tower of Babel (Gen 11:1-9). The first three stories have the same literary pattern—human sin, God's judgment speech, a token of grace, and the execution of God's judgment—that demonstrates persistent human sinfulness, God's determination to judge sin, and also his continuing grace to them.[3]

The Tower of Babel presents a slight but significant departure from the four-part pattern of the other stories in Genesis 3–11. A close look at Genesis 11:1-9 shows that there is no token of grace in this story. The best explanation for the omission is that the Tower of Babel's token of grace is not in the story itself but found in the call of the patriarch Abram:

Go from your country, your people and your father's household
to the land I will show you.

> I will make you into a great nation,
> and I will bless you;
> I will make your name great,
> and you will be a blessing.
> I will bless those who bless you,
> and whoever curses you I will curse;
> and all peoples on earth
> will be blessed through you. (Gen 12:1-3)

Elsewhere, I go into detail on this rich and pivotal passage.[4] Here we must content ourselves by pointing out that this call to Abram (soon renamed Abraham) is God's strategy for reaching reconciliation with his sinful people. Abraham's special status (his election) and that of his descendants (Israel) was not for his or their own privilege but rather for the service of the whole world ("all peoples on earth will be blessed through you"), a service that would lead to suffering.[5]

The book continues by describing the period of the patriarchs (Abraham, Isaac, and Jacob, Gen 12–36), whose colorful stories show the passing down of the promise from father to son. The last portion of the book (Gen 37–50) presents an account that focuses on Jacob's twelve sons, who will become the father figures of the later tribes of Israel (Jacob's second name, Gen 32:22-32), and their actions in this story will affect those tribes' later roles (see Gen 49).

At the end of the book of Genesis, Jacob's family has sought refuge in Egypt because of a devastating famine. The final note indicates an awareness of an ultimate return to the Promised Land (Gen 50:24-26).

The book of Exodus begins some centuries later. The people of God are no longer an extended family but now a bustling population. They are, however, also serving as slaves to the Egyptians.[6] God, though, heard the cry of the enslaved Israelites and sent Moses to lead his people out of Egypt and to the Promised Land. The Israelites were no longer servants to the Pharaoh; they were now servants of their God, who was responding to their cries for help because of his promise to Abraham to make them a "great nation" (Gen 12:2).

Their entry into the Promised Land, though, was delayed due to their persistent complaints in the wilderness. Thus, the generation that left Egypt was condemned to die in the wilderness, and only their children and two faithful spies (Joshua and Caleb; see Num 13–14) could enter the land. And forty years after leaving the land, the Israelites, now under the leadership of Joshua, returned. Joshua led them against the Canaanites, and after their initial push into the Promised Land, they began the settlement. At this time, there were still many Canaanites living there; the Israelites controlled perhaps half of the land.

After the death of Joshua, efforts continued to take more of the land (Judg 1), but soon the Israelites started a pattern of worshiping other gods. In response, God would turn them over to a foreign oppressor, which would ultimately lead the people to turn back to God and cry out to him for help. Then God would raise up a leader (called a judge) who would throw out the foreign oppressor, leading to a period of peace, at least until the next time the people sinned, thus initiating the cycle once again. This period, known as the period of judges, can be characterized as a period of moral depravity, spiritual confusion, and political fragmentation. The book of Judges itself promotes kingship as a cure to this dilemma (Judg 18:1; 19:1; 21:25).

Kingship finally comes to Israel (1 Sam 8–12), but its results were mixed at the beginning and tragic at the end. Saul, the first king, was a disappointment. David, his successor, was about as close to the ideal as anyone came, but he, too, was deeply flawed. The difference between Saul and David was not that the first was sinful and the second was not but rather that David authentically repented when confronted with his sin.[7]

The third king, David's son Solomon, was a turning point. At the start, the book of Kings describes his reign as that of a model, wise monarch. But he ended in disgrace, having had his heart turned toward idolatry by his foreign wives. Thus, his sin led directly to the division of the kingdom into two parts, the North and the South. The book of Kings charts the unfolding of the Northern and Southern Kingdoms with an emphasis on the sins of Israel and Judah and their respective kings. Kings tells us that all of the Northern kings fell short of God's expectations for his leaders (for God's expectations, see Deut 17:14-20). As for the South, led by descendants of David, most were thoroughly corrupt, while others who were not perfect were better in terms of following God. Only two (Hezekiah and Josiah) got high marks for their relationship with and obedience to God.

THE CLOSE BACKGROUND TO THE STORY OF DANIEL

When we come to the divided monarchy, as the period of the split between the Northern and Southern Kingdoms is often called, we are getting closer to the time of Daniel. So, particularly as we come to the end of the period, we need to slow down and give more detail that is relevant to understanding the book of Daniel.

The Northern Kingdom had earlier come to an end in the year 722 BC at the hands of the Assyrians, an empire centered in northern Mesopotamia (today the northern part of Iraq). The Bible gives the divine perspective that it was because of the Israelites' sin that the Assyrians successfully defeated and incorporated them into their growing empire (2 Kings 17).

While the Assyrians did not defeat the Southern Kingdom of Judah, the latter's kings now had to pay tribute to them. But about a century after the Assyrian defeat of the Northern Kingdom, a new power began to arise that threatened Assyrian dominance and eventually the land of Judah. That power was Babylon. Though Babylon had had previous days of glory, over the past couple of centuries it existed as a vassal province of their Northern neighbors, the Assyrians. In 626 BC, though, due to growing Assyrian weakness, an energetic Babylonian leader named Nabopolassar began to assert Babylonian independence.

Nabopolassar. Though Assyria had been weakened by the time of Nabopolassar's rebellion, overthrowing the empire was no easy task and not accomplished overnight. In 612 BC, Babylonian forces, combined with those of the Medes (a power center in western Iran), succeeded in defeating the powerful city of Nineveh, an event anticipated by the prophet Nahum. But even so, Assyria did not disappear. The remnants of Assyrian power fled to the area around Harran in Syria. They were led by a king who took the name Asshur-uballit, meaning, "Assyria lives!" which turned out to be a short-lived and futile hope.

Necho. The next major event in this political and military drama took place in 609 BC. The Egyptian Pharaoh Necho mobilized his armies, presumably out of fear that the growing power of Babylon might eventually threaten their interests in Syria-Palestine and maybe even Egypt itself. Accordingly, Necho marched his army up the coastal highway through Judah and into the province that was formerly the Northern Kingdom of Israel in order to bolster the Assyrian army against the Babylonians. In Judah, Josiah, the faithful king who had reigned since he was a child, took his army up the central hill country route from Jerusalem in order to confront Necho.

Josiah's support for the Babylonian cause was likely fueled by his antipathy toward Assyria, to whom Judah had been paying annual tribute as a vassal since 722 BC. He saw Assyria's downfall as an opportunity for Judah.

Armies, like those of Egypt, marching north along the coastal road, had to jog inland around the city of Megiddo and pass through one of three valleys. Josiah chose that location as the place that was best to ambush the Egyptians. The attack was a short-term disaster and longer-term tragedy for Judah. Not only did they lose, but Josiah, who had led Judah in a God-fearing direction, was killed. According to the book of 2 Chronicles (35:20–36:1), though a faithful king, Josiah had not recognized that it was God's will that Necho go up to fight the Babylonians. The tumultuous history of Judah that follows was the longer-term negative consequence of this defeat.

Necho continued north. He joined the remnants of the Assyrian army, but his help did not lead to victory but rather to defeat in the so-called battle of Carchemish (609 BC). God may have wanted Necho to fight, but apparently so he could lose.

The Assyrians, however, were now finished, leaving an open field for Babylonian expansion to the south. The Egyptians retreated to the south and, though defeated, attempted to stem the Babylonian advance by meddling with the succession of the monarchy in Judah.

When Josiah (640–609 BC) died on the battlefield, his son Jehoahaz assumed the throne (609 BC). But, presumably because Jehoahaz would have continued the pro-Babylonian stance of his father, Necho found a more amenable descendant of David to rule in his place—namely, Josiah's brother Jehoiakim (609–597 BC). With Jehoiakim on the throne, we come to the opening of the book of Daniel (dated to 606/605 BC). In spite of his preference for aligning with Egypt when the Babylonian king put pressure on him, he had no recourse but reluctantly to become a vassal of Babylon. We will later see that much of the action of Daniel 1 relates to Judah's new subordinate status to Babylon.

Nebuchadnezzar. But notice that the Babylonian king is not Nabopolassar but his even more famous son Nebuchadnezzar. Nebuchadnezzar had been crown prince and involved in his father's battles, but in 606/605 BC Nabopolassar died, and Nebuchadnezzar became the king. He would reign for over forty years (until 662 BC), building the empire of Babylon to levels never before achieved in human history.

The reign of Nebuchadnezzar provides the background to the court tales of Daniel 1–4. When commenting on these chapters later, we will see that Daniel has a surprisingly positive attitude toward this great king, particularly when compared to Daniel's dislike of the second major royal figure in the book, Belshazzar. Not only is Belshazzar the king who is on the throne when Daniel has his first two visions (chaps. 7 and 8), he is the king who sees the handwriting on the wall that announces the demise of the Babylonian kingdom (chap. 5).

Time-lapse from Nebuchadnezzar to Belshazzar. From Babylonian sources, we know that a significant time lapse occurs between the end of Nebuchadnezzar's reign (562 BC) and the time Belshazzar rules in Babylon. In between, Babylon had been ruled by Amel-Marduk (562–560 BC), Labashi-Marduk (560–556 BC), Neriglissar (556 BC), and finally Nabonidus (556–539 BC). Indeed, according to Babylonian king lists, Nabonidus was the last king of Babylon. For many years, the mention of Belshazzar in the book of Daniel was thought to be a historical error.

That is, until we received more information.

About seventy-five years ago, ancient cuneiform tablets were discovered that mentioned a king named Bel-shar-usur, the son of Nabonidus. Nabonidus was an idiosyncratic ruler of Babylon. While Marduk was the chief deity of the Babylonian pantheon, Nabonidus's family was from a region that worshiped the moon god Sin. Indeed, Nabonidus worshiped Sin and ignored the worship of Marduk, which brought the anger of the powerful Marduk priesthood and the people. Nabonidus eventually relocated his palace to an oasis in what today is

Saudi Arabia (Tayma) and ruled from there. He then set his son, our Belshazzar, as his coregent, on the throne in Babylon. Thus, it is Belshazzar, not Nabonidus, who was the recipient of the message written on the wall.[8]

EXCURSUS:
Daniel 4 and the Prayer of Nabonidus (*4QPrNab*)

Speaking of Nabonidus, we should take a look at the so-called Prayer of Nabonidus often brought into discussions of the historical reliability of the book of Daniel. Later (see chap. 6) we will take a closer look at the message of Daniel 4, where we will read about how King Nebuchadnezzar suffers a seven-year period of madness in which he will act and think like an animal. Four fragments of an original text were discovered at Qumran and published in 1956 that contain a strikingly similar story to that found in Daniel 4 but with a significant differ-ence noted in the next paragraph. The fragments, dated to between 75–50 BC but perhaps a copy of an earlier story, talk about a Babylonian king who suffered from a seven-year madness where he "became comparable [with the beasts]."[9] A Jewish diviner then interprets the cause of the madness as the king's worship of idols. The resolution comes when the king states: "Then I prayed before God, and [as for] my offense—he forgave it." (Notice that the king is the first-person speaker of the prayer like Nebuchadnezzar is the first-person speaker in Daniel 4.)

This story, while having remarkable correspondence with Daniel 4, is different in that the beast-like king is Nabonidus in the Qumran text and Nebuchadnezzar in Daniel. What we make of the relationship between these two texts depends on a host of factors.

Perhaps the Nabonidus story is the earliest version of the story of a king becoming animal-like, and the author of Daniel changed the name to Nebuchadnezzar because that

king played such a significant role as the king who destroyed Jerusalem and exiled its leading citizens.[10] After all,
the historical Nabonidus was known to make some decisions that would have been considered bizarre by others.
Strangely for his time, he worshiped only one god, the moon
god, even neglecting the support of the main god of the
Babylonians, Marduk.

On the other hand, perhaps the story moved the other way,
with the Nebuchadnezzar story first and the name of the king
being changed to Nabonidus. A third possibility strikes me as
extremely unlikely, which is that they both experienced the
same strange mental illness.

The bottom line is that we can't know for sure the exact
relationship between these two ancient texts.

But neither Daniel's story nor the historical issues associated with it
come to an end with the close of the Babylonian Empire. Daniel lives
on into the first few years of the Persian Empire that succeeded
the Babylonians.

Both the Bible and other contemporary ancient Near Eastern sources
inform us that Belshazzar's (and Nabonidus's) Babylon falls to the
mighty Persian Empire. The Persian Empire, which like the Medes
whom they absorbed, was a nation-state that had its center in western
Iran. Among its major cities was Susa.

The Bible and other ancient Near Eastern sources name the conquering king Cyrus, often called the Great. Cyrus is indeed mentioned
as the ruler at the time of Daniel's fourth and final vision (chaps. 10–12,
see 10:1), but the book of Daniel raises questions when it names
someone called Darius the Mede as the one who took over the kingdom
(Dan 5:31) and as the one who was ruling in Babylon at the time that
Daniel was thrown into the lions' den (chap. 6). He is also named
(Darius son of Xerxes [a Mede by descent], 9:1) as the ruler at the time
of Daniel's prayer and message from the angel Gabriel. Who is Darius
the Mede?

Darius the Mede. The book presents Darius the Mede as the ruler of Babylon at the beginning of the Persian period. The problem is that according to all other records, biblical and ancient Near Eastern, that position belongs rather to Cyrus.

One solution proposed by some is that the mention of Darius the Mede is simply a historical error. A number of scholars believe that the book of Daniel was composed long after the sixth century BC, the setting of the events of the book of Daniel, and that Darius the Mede is simply a mistake generated by the distance of time between its setting and when the book was actually written. (See below on the debate concerning the time of the composition of the book.) As H. H. Rowley put it in 1935, Darius the Mede was the result of the "conflation of confused traditions."[11] Others, including myself, don't want to be hasty in such a conclusion, especially considering how the mystery surrounding Belshazzar ultimately was solved with more information.

Thus, there are various possible explanations put forward on the basis of the knowledge that we have presently, though it would be mistaken to give the impression that any of these ideas are widely accepted. These explanations begin with the recognition of the well-attested practice of giving kings a different throne name in the various parts of the empire in which they ruled. A biblical example of this is when the well-known Assyrian king Tiglath-Pileser III is called "Pul" in 1 Chronicles 5:26. This raises the possibility that Darius the Mede was a second name given to a person whom we might know by another name.

A number of candidates have been put forward as possibilities that might be identified with Darius the Mede. Perhaps Darius the Mede is actually Gubaru, whom we know from texts written in Akkadian as the governor of Babylon under Cyrus.[12] Another theory identifies Darius the Mede as the Babylonian throne name of none other than Cyrus the Great.[13] If this were the case, then we would translate Daniel 6:28 as "Daniel prospered in the reign of Darius, even [rather than *and*] Cyrus the Persian." Recently, Anderson and Young have reasserted the view that there is a Darius who would have been contemporary with Daniel and the defeat of Babylon that is mentioned in a couple of obscure references. The citations are allusive and enigmatic, though, and have failed to persuade many scholars.[14]

These and other hypotheses have been put forward to try to solve the question of the identity of Darius the Mede, but as we have already admitted, none are conclusive.[15] But rather than taking this question as evidence against the historical reality of Darius, we should, in my opinion, reserve judgment pending further information.

Cyrus the Great. Finally, we come to Cyrus the Great. We have already considered the possibility that Cyrus and Darius the Mede are one and the same, but we are not at all certain about this. What we do know is that Daniel survived into the beginning of his reign (Dan 1:21; 6:28) and that Daniel had his last vision in that king's third year (Dan 10:1). Cyrus was named "Great" by tradition because he was the one who brought various tribal/national elements in western Iran (particularly the Persians and Medes) together to form a powerful core that then expanded its empire by defeating Lydia, a power in Asia Minor and then Babylon, which brought that entire empire under its sway.

The book of Isaiah views Cyrus very positively (Is 44:28; 45:1, 13). After all, he conquered Babylon, which had subjugated Judah and deported its leading citizens. Judah, now referred to as Yehud, remained a province under the dominance of Persia, but Cyrus initiated a different foreign policy that allowed more autonomy among its friendly vassals. The end of 2 Chronicles (2 Chron 36:22-23) and the beginning of Ezra (Ezra 1:1-4) both record the so-called Cyrus Decree that allowed the Jews who were exiled by the Babylonians to return to their homeland.[16]

As the book of Esther, set in the time of the later Persian king Xerxes, indicates, not all Jewish people decided to return. It is likely that the aged Daniel did not choose to return. He almost certainly died soon after Cyrus achieved his great military and political victories.

BACKGROUND TO DANIEL'S VISIONS

Thus, Daniel lived during the late seventh and deep into the sixth century BC. The action of the book starts with the subjugation of

Jerusalem by the Babylonians (around 606/05 BC) and the last recorded time is the third year of Cyrus (around 537/36 BC). That said, Daniel's visions look further into the future. At this point, we will just speak in terms of generalities, but when we look at specific visions in later chapters, we will give more detail.

Cyrus's defeat of Babylon (539 BC) initiated what today is typically called the Persian period. This period of time lasted until 331 BC, when Alexander (also referred to as "the Great") defeated the last Persian emperor, Darius III, at the battle of Gaugamela. The young Alexander (he was twenty-five at the time), the king of the Greek kingdom of Macedonia, incorporated the vast Persian Empire and extended it to the Indus Valley. Alexander died relatively soon after his last victory (323 BC). Since his heir was young, the kingdom was temporarily divided into four parts and placed under the rulership of one of his leading generals. These generals never gave up their power and thus established their own dynasties.

Since their origins were Greek, the next era in the Near East is often referred to as the Hellenistic period. The eastern region of Alexander's kingdom was divided between two of Alexander's powerful generals. In the north, with its capital in the Syrian city of Antioch, Seleucus established a dynasty, while in the south, with its capital in the newly built city of Alexandria, Ptolemy and his descendants ruled. Jerusalem was located between these two great kingdoms, and dominance of Jerusalem and the region was a matter of contention between the Seleucid and Ptolemaic kingdoms. We will see that these kings provide the background for the detailed prophecies of various "kings of the North" (Seleucid) and "kings of the South" (Ptolemaic) in Daniel 11.

For some who date the composition of the book of Daniel in the second century BC, these Hellenistic kingdoms provide the endpoint of Daniel's visions, but for others, the vision extends to the next great world empire (and beyond), Rome. Rome extended its influence in the region beginning in the second century BC but incorporated Jerusalem after a siege by Pompey in 63 BC. Judah was a province of Rome at the time of Jesus.

THE DATE OF COMPOSITION OF THE BOOK OF DANIEL

Many readers of the book of Daniel may be surprised to realize that the question of its date of composition is one of the most contentious issues in biblical studies. The reason why it is often fiercely debated is because, in the mind of some scholars who date the book to around the time of Daniel's life, the very integrity of the book is at issue, while in the minds of others, the book shows obvious signs of being written later. In this section, we will lay out the arguments, point out what is at stake, and make a case for the earlier date while also acknowledging the problems with such a position.

As we observed earlier in the chapter, the book of Daniel presents itself as describing events that take place in the very late seventh and early sixth centuries. Now, of course, a later author could have written stories about Daniel and even included accounts of Daniel's vision. The book itself does not tell us who wrote the final form or even who wrote the stories that might have been passed down in written and oral form before being included in what we know as the book of Daniel. Interestingly, even the visions, which are described by Daniel in the first person ("I, Daniel"), sometimes have a third-person ("He, Daniel") introduction. This is true of the first and the last visions (Dan 7:1; 10:1), but not of the two middle visions (8:1; 9:2). Still a case could be made that a later author produced the final form of the book.

The debate arises, though, when the argument for the late date of the composition of the book suggests that the visions in chapters 7–12 that are presented as looking into Daniel's future are really written after the events that they purport to prophecy. In other words, they are not true prophecies, but rather they are prophecies after the fact. To those who believe that the book of Daniel is the Word of God and thus does not mislead its readers, this type of writing seems to lack integrity, though as we will see there are some authors who try to get around this charge.

So we can see that the debate is really focused on the date of the visions themselves, not necessarily on when those visions were incorporated into the book as we have it. Did a historical sixth-century Daniel have visions that looked into the future, or were these visions constructed by someone much later after the majority of the events happened and then attributed to an earlier figure named Daniel (who may or may not be an actual person)?

But now let's lay out the main features of the two main views of the date of the writing of the book.

Early date of the book. Those who advocate for an early date of the writing of the book, or at least an early date for the sources that inform the book, believe that it reflects a reliable picture of Daniel and his friends in the late seventh and early sixth centuries BC and report actual visions that predate the events that they describe. This view was the predominant view by far until the rise of the historical-critical approach in the aftermath of the Enlightenment.[17] Historical criticism at its core denies or at least brackets the supernatural universe. The so-called principle of analogy, for instance, argues that if something does not happen today, then we cannot believe it happened in antiquity. If seas don't split today, then we must disbelieve that they split in the past. If people do not predict future events through special divine revelation today, then we must not suppose they did in the past.[18] Sibley Towner well represents this historical-critical mindset when he says:

> We need to assume that the vision as a whole is a prophecy after the fact. Why? Because human beings are unable accurately to predict future events centuries in advance and to say that Daniel could do so, even on the basis of a symbolic revelation vouchsafed to him by God and interpreted by an angel, is to fly in the face of the certainties of human nature. So what we have here is in fact not a road map of the future laid down in the sixth century B.C. but an interpretation of the events of the author's own time, 167–164 B.C.[19]

In a sense, the traditional approach to the dating of the contents of the book of Daniel thus represents the default position that was held until the advent of the historical-critical approach. It takes the book at its word (or so it seems at least on the surface). Accordingly, rather than presenting a case for the dating (which seems self-evident), those of us who exert our efforts in defending the early date spend our efforts answering arguments that dispute it (as in the next section).

Late date of the book. For many scholars like Towner, the late date is obvious since such detailed prophecies of future events are impossible for humans who have limited understanding of the future. Perhaps particularly perceptive humans can detect future trends in the near future, but the kind of detailed prophecies that Daniel gives, particularly in chapter 11, are beyond human ability.

Those of us who believe, along with the apostle Peter, that "prophecy never had its origin in the human will, but prophets, though human, spoke from God as they were carried along by the Holy Spirit" (2 Pet 1:21), will find such an argument unconvincing to be sure. God knows the future and can reveal it to his people if he chooses. Indeed, according to Isaiah, God's ability to know the future is precisely what differentiates him from false gods (Is 41:25-29; 42:8-9; 44:6-8). However, there is a further twist to this argument that should be recognized as problematic even for those of us who have no problem with God revealing the future to his servants the prophets.

Thus, unless one either does not believe, or for academic reasons brackets their belief, in a God who can speak truly about the future in as much detail as we find in Daniel 11, the "Towner argument" is a nonstarter. But not everyone who accepts the late date for Daniel takes this approach. Indeed, a number of scholars with a very high view of the Bible as the Word of God have lately argued for a similar position but on different grounds.

Their approach typically goes something like the following. The book of Daniel is an apocalyptic book. Most nonbiblical apocalyptic books were written after the time of their purportedly predicted events (the technical term is *vaticinium ex eventu*) by unknown authors who took on the name of a well-known worthy (the technical term is *pseudonymous*). Thus, Daniel is a well-known type of literature for its ancient context and thus would not be fooling anyone. The original audience would know that it is pseudonymous and written after the fact, so if judged by its contemporary standards, it is a reliable book.

There is much about this line of argument that must be appreciated.[20] We should read biblical books in their ancient context and not impose modern standards on them. And this approach rightly characterizes many nonbiblical apocalypses.

First Enoch is a collection of writings including apocalypses that were likely written between the fourth and first centuries BC. The visions, however, purport to come from Enoch, the prediluvian figure mentioned in the genealogy in Genesis 5 who did not die but whom "God took . . . away" (Gen 5:24). In 1 Enoch he relates revelations that he received in a heavenly journey to his son Methuselah. This book clearly does contain prophecy after the fact and is pseudonymous.

The problem that remains, however, is that the authors of books like 1 Enoch were intentionally trying to deceive their readers. It is simply not true that their contemporary readers were aware that these were prophecies after the fact. These books only achieve their goals through the deception of their audiences. They are attempting to convince their readers that they have the prophetic gift by pretending to have predicted events that have already happened in order to, at the end, present an actual prediction of the future.

Scholars like John Goldingay also point to a genre of texts written in Akkadian that are clearly pseudonymous, including some texts that end with prophecy, which some call apocalyptic to create the possibility of similarity with the book of Daniel.[21] These texts include the Marduk Prophecy, the Shulgi Prophecy, the Uruk Prophecy, Text A, and the Dynastic Prophecy.[22] We will mention the Dynastic Prophecy again when we come to our study of Daniel 11 since these two texts share a similar style and format. Goldingay believes that the pseudonymous nature and after-the-fact prophecy that he argues the book of Daniel shares with these Akkadian texts would have been familiar and known to the original audience since we have a number of examples. But again the problem is that these other texts all only work in their intention if they actually fool their original audience into believing they are real prophecies.

Since these texts traffic in deception, those of us who think that the book of Daniel is the Word of God find it hard to conclude that Daniel shares these traits since it would involve God in that deception. That said, we do have to recognize a difficulty with the opinion that Daniel is prophecy before the fact because in one case, it looks, at least on the surface, as if there is a failed prophecy at the end of Daniel 11.

I will give the details later, but Daniel 11 presents a prophecy that begins in the Persian period but focuses in the Greek period, speaking of the actions and interaction between kings of the North (the Seleucids) and kings of the South (Ptolemies). At the end of chapter 11, we will give attention to a particularly brutal king of the South whom we know as Antiochus Epiphanes. As we will see later in chapter 13, at first the prophecies agree with what we know about this king, but at the end when it speaks of his death, it does not seem to accurately reflect what we know from other historical records. Therefore, some conclude that the author accurately "prophecies" events up to his present, but then when he makes an attempt at "real" prophecy, he fails.

While we have to admit we have an issue to be resolved here in defense of the idea that this prophecy originated with a historical Daniel in the sixth century BC, we can also see the theological-ethical problem with the idea that Daniel 11 is a prophecy after the fact. After gaining the readers' trust for accurately describing events that will take place after the death of Daniel up to the final moment, then the author attempts to provide a prophecy that fails.

My own view on this matter is that either Daniel gave this prophecy and that it didn't actually fail or Daniel 11 trades in deception and then concludes with a false prophecy. I believe the former and will provide an interpretation of the end of Daniel 11 in chapter 13 that preserves its integrity.

CONCLUSION

Daniel, like all biblical literature, must be read with an awareness of its original historical context. All biblical books were written with a contemporary audience in mind, and Daniel is no exception to this observation. Thus, it is important to know: (1) the biblical history that leads up to the time of Daniel; (2) the historical background to the events behind the book of Daniel; (3) and something about the original date of composition.

DISCUSSION QUESTIONS

1. Give a brief summary of the story given by the Bible's historical narrative from the time of the creation up to the time of Daniel.

2. Give a short description of the events that take place in the background of the action in the book of Daniel.

3. What are the two major views of when the book of Daniel was written? Which do you find more persuasive?

THREE

Comfort in the Midst of Oppression

The Theme of the Book

A t first glance, the book of Daniel seems to be more like a collection than a unified literary composition. We have seen how there are two main types of literature in the book, court tales in chapters 1–6 and apocalyptic visions in chapters 7–12. And these chapters are even written in two different languages, Hebrew (1:1–2:4a; 8–12) and Aramaic (2:4b–7:28). But in this chapter, we will see that, though diverse in language and style, these six court tales and four apocalyptic visions have a single coherent theme: in spite of present difficulties, God is in control, and he will have the final victory.

We will wait to give a detailed exposition of this theme until we come to the chapters that interpret the various tales and visions, but here we will present the theme in general with just a few examples. We will also see that there is a second theme or message that was relevant for the original readers of the book: "God's people can survive and even thrive in the midst of a toxic culture."

PRIMARY THEME: IN SPITE OF PRESENT DIFFICULTIES, GOD IS IN CONTROL, AND HE WILL HAVE THE FINAL VICTORY

In spite of present difficulties. God's people find themselves in difficult straits right from the first verses of the book of Daniel. As a result of a Babylonian siege, the king of Jerusalem submits to Nebuchadnezzar's authority and becomes a vassal state of his vast and growing empire.

Judah's king, Jehoiakim, had to turn over "some of the articles from the temple of God" (Dan 1:2) to be placed in the temple of Nebuchad-nezzar's god in Babylon. Further, he had to send some of the young nobles to Babylon to serve in his foreign court. While all of Judah was under the authority of Babylon from this point on, the book focuses particularly on the fate of Daniel and his three friends, political hos-tages who must live in the court of Babylon, an environment that was toxic to their faith in Yahweh, the true God.

Their lives, as faithful men in a pagan court, are troubled, and com-plications arise at every turn. They must study "the language and lit-erature of the Babylonians" and eat "royal food and wine" that would somehow "defile" them (1:4, 8). In chapter 2, Daniel and his friends live under the threat of death if they are unable to tell the king his dream and interpret it. Chapter 3 focuses on Daniel's three friends, who refuse to bow to a gigantic golden statue that Nebuchadnezzar set up in the plain of Dura. In chapter 4, Daniel takes a risk in interpreting a dream of this powerful king that turns out to be a threat to the king himself and his empire. In chapter 5, Daniel again must interpret a negative message for a foreign king, this time the insecure Belshazzar, and in chapter 6, Daniel is thrown into a den of lions for continuing to pray to the true God.

The imagery of the four visions also show that the people of God were living in a hostile environment that threatened their lives and faith. In the first vision, the difficulties are symbolized by four horri-fying sea beasts, the ten horns on the fourth beast, and ultimately by the little horn that speaks boastfully (Dan 7). In the second vision, conflict is symbolized again by violent animals, in this case a ram and a goat (Dan 8). In the third vision, Daniel receives a divine message that in essence says that the seventy-year exile announced by the prophet Jeremiah will not yet come to a definitive end; more suffering is to come (Dan 9). And then in the lengthy fourth vision (Dan 10:1–12:3), we hear of the fight between various kings of the North and kings of the South, culminating in the atrocities of one particular king of the South who will horribly persecute the people of God.

All six court tales and four visions begin with the people of God in precarious situations. As they look around, all they see is trouble. Evil people who want to harm them have the upper hand. There does not seem to be a way out. But the message of the book of Daniel is not interested in simply naming their risk but in reminding them that behind the scenes God is still in control.

God is in control. On the ground, the situation was dire. God's people were living under the thrall of the most powerful empires that humanity has ever seen—Babylon, Persia, and Greece. They had lost their independent kingdom to Babylon and then became a part of Babylon's successors thereafter.

God's people themselves were scattered. The leading citizens had been exiled to Babylon in 597 and 586 BC. But many, indeed the majority of the people, remained in Judah under the rule of a foreign-appointed Jewish governor.

True, at the very end of Daniel's life, the Persians, who displaced the Babylonians as overlords of the region, allowed the exiles to return, but not all, perhaps not even the majority, chose to do so but chose, like Mordecai and Esther (see the book of Esther), to remain a part of the diaspora (Greek for "scattering").

The book of Daniel itself speaks little beyond the experience of Daniel and his three friends. But their story well illustrates the truth behind the surface reality—namely, that God is in control. This message is meant to provide comfort to all of God's people who read these stories and visions who are living in cultures that are toxic to their faith. We will later see that this refers to all of us, even in the twenty-first century AD (see chap. 15).

As we observed in the previous section, the opening verses of the book narrate the Babylonians' successful siege of Jerusalem. On the ground, the Babylonians seem to be in control. The book's narrator, though, pulls aside the curtains and tells us that "the Lord delivered Jehoiakim king of Judah into his [Nebuchadnezzar's] hand" (Dan 1:2). In other words, Babylon's victory was not the result of the Babylonians' superior power but because God allowed it to happen.

Interestingly, the narrator is not interested, at this point at least, in speaking about the reason why God allowed this to happen. Reading the history of Israel and Judah (particularly the book of Kings in the light of Deuteronomy) and the prophets that preceded the various defeats of Israel and Judah (see for instance, Isaiah, Jeremiah, and Ezekiel as well as a number of the so-called Minor Prophets), there is no doubt but that God allowed the taking of Jerusalem as a vassal to happen because of the people's disobedience.

The book of Daniel, however, was not written to remind the Jewish people of their sin but to provide encouragement to them in the midst of their oppression. The focus is on God's control, not his punishment.

For this reason, in all the trouble that follows in chapters 2–6, God shows that he is in control. In the first chapter, Daniel and his three friends (Hananiah, Mishael, and Azariah) end up looking the best in their physical appearance in spite of the fact that they eat vegetables and drink water rather than the diet provided by the court. God reveals the content and interpretation of the king's dream in Daniel 2. God sends his angel to save the three friends from the fiery furnace in Daniel 3. God reveals the meaning of Nebuchadnezzar's second dream in Daniel 4. God's control over world powers becomes clear when he announces the demise of Babylon through his writing a message on the wall of Belshazzar's palace in Daniel 5. And God shuts the mouths of the ravenous lions in Daniel 6.

The four visions also powerfully communicate that in spite of present difficulties, God is in control.

In Daniel 7, after the vision of the four beasts rising out of the sea, the scene shifts to a courtroom and the Ancient of Days, a figure that clearly represents God in his role as judge. While we will consider the details of this impressive scene in a later chapter, we can see right from the start that God is in control of the situation.

The second vision (Dan 8) also speaks of God's control, though the majority of the chapter concerns the havoc caused by the two nations represented by the ram and the goat and the powers that derive from them. Indeed, the vision culminates by describing the terrors perpetrated by "a fierce-looking king, a master of intrigue" (Dan 8:23), who will even challenge the "Prince of princes" (Dan 8:25). But then when we read, "Yet he will be destroyed, but not by human power" (Dan 8:25), we know that God is the one who is in control.

The message of Daniel 9 is somewhat different, as we will see in a later chapter (12). In response to Daniel's prayer calling for an end to the exile, God sends Gabriel to Daniel with a message that "seventy 'sevens' are decreed for your people" (Dan 9:24). As we will see, the upshot of this decree is that the exile will continue, but notice that the decree shows that it is God who is in control of these future events.

The lengthy final vision has a similar message as the first two because it describes the horrors of powerful human kingdoms ravaging God's people. In chapter 8, for example, the vision ends with one particularly ruthless royal figure, who even challenges God ("he will exalt and magnify himself above every god and will say unheard-of things against the God of gods" [Dan 11:36]). But, as Gabriel informs Daniel, this king will "come to his end, and no one will help him" (Dan 11:45).

In addition, the book of Daniel demonstrates God's control over an evil and chaotic world through the use of symbolic numbers and references to periods of time in the context of the visions. In Daniel 7, we hear that the first three beasts representing evil human kingdoms "were allowed to live for a period of time" (Dan 7:12). Later in the chapter, we learn that the "holy people" will be oppressed, but notice there is a time limit given by the interpreting angel that is intentionally obscure; it is said that they will be "delivered into his hands for a time, times and half a time" (Dan 7:25), after which time the oppressor will be destroyed.

In Daniel 8, where we learn that a little horn that grew in power will oppress the people of God and violate the sanctuary, we also are informed that this profanation will be limited since the sanctuary will be reconsecrated after "2,300 evenings and mornings" (Dan 8:14). Daniel 9 has perhaps the most enigmatic as well as best-known references to time when it announces that the seventy-year exile spoken of by Jeremiah is said to now be a period of "seventy 'sevens'" (Dan 9:24-27) until "the end that is decreed is poured out on him [the final oppressor]" (Dan 9:27).

We will mention just one more example, this one appearing at the very end of the book. Daniel has been told that the oppression that God's people have been experiencing will continue, but that it will come to an end. He asks the natural question: "How long will it be before these astonishing things are fulfilled?" (Dan 12:6). The answer again comes in the form of enigmatic numbers, "It will be for a time, times and half a time. When the power of the holy people has been finally broken, all these things will be completed" (Dan 12:7). Then a little later we read, "From the time that the daily sacrifice is abolished and the abomination that causes desolation is set up, there will be 1,290 days. Blessed is the one who waits for and reaches the end of the 1,335 days" (Dan 12:11-12).

Later, we will examine these numbers much more closely, but even then we will see that they remain enigmatic and should not be treated as signals that need to be translated to an apocalyptic timetable that counts down to the end of time. For now, I want to simply point out that these numbers are the author's way of saying, "Things look out of control, but they are really not." God will end the oppression on his schedule. God is indeed in control, even if the reader cannot know precisely when the events will happen.

So now we know that, in spite of present difficulties, God is indeed in control. But the message goes on beyond God's control of the situation. The book of Daniel announces clearly—God will have the final victory.

And he will have the final victory. The Babylonians defeated Judah and exiled its leading citizens, beginning with young nobles like Daniel and his three friends. Babylon reduced Judah from vassal status to a province within its empire in 586 BC, and Judah would continue to be a province in the empires that succeeded Babylon.

Even so, as we recounted in the previous section, God was in control. He allowed this subjugation to take place. But the message of the book of Daniel importantly goes beyond the announcement that God is in control. The wonderful news that the book communicates to its faithful readers is that God will have the final victory. Again, we will explain the details of the various chapters of the book of Daniel in the next section of this book, but we will anticipate the main message here.

In Daniel 1, at the end of their training to enter the king's service, we see that they not only survived, but the king "found them ten times better than all the magicians and enchanters in his whole kingdom" (Dan 1:20).

In Daniel 2, God shows his control through revealing the content of Nebuchadnezzar's dream to Daniel. The dream itself describes God's ultimate victory over the evil human kingdoms represented by the metals of the statue when we see the destruction of the statue by a "rock cut out of a mountain, but not by human hands" (Dan 2:45). In chapter 3, God kept the three friends safe from the fire. Even Nebuchadnezzar himself celebrated God's victory (Dan 3:28-29)!

In the next chapter (Dan 4), in spite of warning, Nebuchadnezzar's achievements go to his head, and he revels in his unsurpassed power. God then reduces his mind to that of an animal until he acknowledged that the "God Most High" was supreme.

In chapter 5, Belshazzar, the last Babylonian king, blasphemed the true God while praising his false gods using the goblets that were looted from the temple by Nebuchadnezzar (Dan 1:2). But God will not be mocked by this puffed-up monarch, and after announcing the end of the Babylonian kingdom through the writing on the wall, the Persians defeated him and took over the kingdom. Belshazzar "did not honor the God who holds in his hand your life and all your ways" (Dan 5:23), so God removed him.

Chapter 6 shares affinities with chapter 3, but Daniel, rather than the three friends, is the main protagonist. Due to false charges by jealous colleagues, King Darius has Daniel thrown into a lions' den. God shows his control by having his angelic agent keep the mouths of the lions shut. Daniel survived the night, but when his accusers were thrown in the den with their families, they did not even hit the floor of the den before the lions ripped them apart. God had the victory, and Darius celebrates him: "He rescues and he saves; he performs signs and wonders in the heavens and on the earth. He has rescued Daniel from the power of the lions" (Dan 6:27).

As in the tales, so the visions announce God's ultimate victory.

Daniel 7 not only shows that God is in control as the Ancient of Days announces judgment against the evil kingdoms represented by the beasts and the horns of the fourth beast. The final word of the interpretation of Daniel's dream is that the final evil king will have his power taken away, "Then the sovereignty, power and greatness of all the kingdoms under heaven will be handed over to the holy people of the Most High. His kingdom will be an everlasting kingdom, and all rulers will worship and obey him" (Dan 7:27).

We have already noted that God's control, as well as his final victory, is subtly but clearly announced in chapter eight by the statement that the "fierce-looking king, a master of intrigue . . . will be destroyed, but not by human power" (Dan 8:23, 25). Daniel 9 is also subtle in its announcement of God's ultimate victory. As we will see in a later chapter, much remains obscure, probably intentionally so, in Gabriel's statement about the "seventy 'sevens,'" but in spite of the atrocities that will occur during this time, they will come to an end because the evil figure who perpetrates so much harm will continue to do damage "until the end that is decreed is poured out on him" (Dan 9:27).

The final vision, we have seen, describes again the evil kingdoms of this world that rise up and oppress God's people. In this vision, the emphasis is on the Greek period, when Jerusalem is caught between the competing Seleucid rulers in the north and the Ptolemies in the south. The final focus is on a particularly egregious king of the North, whom we will later identify as Antiochus Epiphanes IV but whose profile, we will argue, bleeds into a final antichrist figure. But this climactic representative of the evil that oppresses God's people and even challenges God himself "will come to his end" (Dan 11:45), and ultimately God's victory will issue forth when "multitudes who sleep in the dust of the earth will awake: some to everlasting life, others to shame and everlasting contempt" (Dan 12:2).

Comfort in the midst of oppression. We have begun our study of Daniel with an initial survey of the twelve chapters to highlight the book's main theme: in spite of present difficulties, God is in control, and he will have the final victory. A more detailed look at these chapters is soon to follow, but I want to first take a broad-lensed look at the book to discover this theme to guide our more detailed exposition, even though this theme arose out of our close look at the book.

Before moving on, we should recognize the importance of this theme to Daniel's contemporary audience, and at the end of the chapter, we will reflect on how this importance continues to the present day. Whether the book comes out of the experiences of the sixth century or the second century (see chapter 2 on the dating of the book's composition), the people of God were under the stern control of foreign powers that had animosity toward the faith of the faithful. They were living in a toxic and dangerous culture, and they had no control over their situation.

The book of Daniel is intended to bring comfort to these faithful, oppressed people. As they surveyed their world, it looked like their oppressors were in control. The temptation would be to think that the gods of their oppressors were more powerful than their God. The book of Daniel pulls back the curtains and points out that in reality God is in control and he will have the final victory. Stay faithful in spite of your present pain and trouble.

SECONDARY THEME: GOD'S PEOPLE CAN SURVIVE AND EVEN THRIVE IN THE MIDST OF A TOXIC CULTURE

In spite of present difficulties, God is in control and will have the final victory. This message encourages God's people to remain confident in the midst of their present struggles. But there is a message beyond the encouragement to live in a difficult present with hope, as important as that message is. Daniel and his three friends not only survived their ordeals and lived knowing that at some future time, probably after their lifetime, God would give his people victory over their oppressors. They also experienced success in their lives, thanks to God.

We can see this theme illustrated in both the praise that they receive from their overlords as well as their frequent promotions in the court. At the end of their training in preparation to serve in Nebuchadnezzar's court, we hear that the king "found them ten times better than all the magicians and enchanters in his whole kingdom" (Dan 1:20). When Daniel told Nebuchadnezzar the content of his dream and interpreted it, "The king placed Daniel in a high position and lavished many gifts on him. He made him ruler over the entire province of Babylon and placed him in charge of all its wise men" (Dan 2:48). Shadrach, Meshach, and Abed-Nego, his friends called here by their Babylonian names, also were appointed to high positions.

After these three friends survived the fiery furnace, they were further promoted (Dan 3:30). After correctly interpreting the significance of the writing on the wall, Belshazzar commanded that Daniel be "proclaimed the third highest ruler in the kingdom" (Dan 5:29). Daniel's promotions brought on the jealous anger of his pagan peers at the beginning of the Persian period. They tricked Darius into condemning Daniel to death by being thrown in the lions' den. After he survived the ordeal, the account ends by saying, "Daniel prospered during the reign of Darius and the reign of Cyrus the Persian" (Dan 6:28).

Again, the message of these first six chapters is clear to God's people who find themselves in a culture that is toxic to their faith. Stay faithful no matter what. And know that you too can not only survive but thrive in an oppressive culture.

We should be quick to point out, though, that this is not a promise or a guarantee. God calls his people to remain faithful even if it means that they might suffer or even die. The three friends realized this when they were given the option of bowing to Nebuchadnezzar's statue to prevent being thrown into the fire. At this point, they do not know that God will save them, but still, they stay faithful even if it means their death: "If we are thrown into the blazing furnace, the God we serve is able to deliver us from it, and he will deliver us from Your Majesty's hand. But even if he does not, we want you to know, Your Majesty, that we will not serve your gods or worship the image of gold you have set up" (Dan 3:17-18).

CONCLUSION

The book of Daniel has two main parts; the first (chaps. 1–6) contains six stories, and the second (chaps. 7–12) contains four apocalyptic visions. While different in many ways, all six stories and all four apocalyptic visions share the same important message for its readers who live in a culture toxic to their faith. First, in spite of present circumstances, God is in control and will have the final victory. In addition, the faithful learn that not only can people survive but they can also thrive in the midst of such a toxic culture. Therefore, the main purpose of the book of Daniel is to comfort God's people in the midst of trouble.

Finally, I want to point out that these two themes make explicit that the book of Daniel, while not advocating open rebellion against the political powers that exploit them, implicitly resist them. Daniel and his three friends do not cower to the powerful kings that rule these empires nor to the elites that serve them. They know true power lies with God, and that is whom they will worship and serve.[1]

DISCUSSION QUESTIONS

1. Express and discuss the main theme: in spite of difficulty, God is in control and will have the final victory. Choose one chapter in the book of Daniel and illustrate how it works out.

2. Express and discuss the second theme: one can not only survive but thrive in a toxic culture. Choose one chapter in the book of Daniel and illustrate how it works out.

3. Can you see how the message of these stories and apocalyptic visions can comfort the troubled people of God? Can they provide comfort for Christians today?

PART 2

Reading Daniel as Six Stories and Four Visions

In part one, we did an overview of Daniel from a literary (chap. 1), historical (chap. 2), and theological perspective (chap. 3). Now in part two, we turn to a closer inspection of the six stories and four apocalyptic visions that are included in the book, all of which individually illustrate the same major theme: in spite of present difficulties, God is in control, and he will have the final victory.

We will begin with a study of the six stories that are found in Daniel 1–6. As we observed above, these chapters may be divided into two main types: tales of court contest and tales of court conflict. In both cases, Daniel and his three friends usually find themselves at odds with their foreign colleagues. In the former, the Hebrew wise men demonstrate abilities that far surpass those of the Babylonian wise men. Indeed, at least in Daniel 1–2, the success of Daniel and his friends rescued the Babylonian wise men from death. As the name of the latter suggests, the tales of court conflict introduce hostility between the two parties. In these stories, the Babylonian wise men want to kill Daniel and/or the three friends.

On the surface, all these stories make Daniel and his friends look good over against the Babylonian wise men. But as we take a closer look we will see that in reality, these accounts don't make them look good, they rather point to God's superior wisdom and power.

In chapters 4–7, we treat the tales of court contest first before the tales of court conflict, and there are three such stories (Dan 1–2, 4, and 5) if we understand, as I think we should, Daniel 1 and 2 together. True, Daniel 1 can stand on its own as a discrete story with its own plot, and the same is true for the second chapter. Even so, as I hope to show in chapter four of the present book, there is a tight connection between Daniel 1 and 2. So while I think it is true that chapter one is an introduction to all the tales of the first part of Daniel and maybe even of the entire book, in another way it has a special connection with chapter two.

After investigating the message of these first two connected chapters, we will turn our attention to the other two tales of court contest (Dan 4 and 5), and we will see that they, too, have a special relationship with each other.

These are stories about Daniel without the three friends. In both cases, we will see that there is an enigmatic message from God given to the Babylonian king, which he is unable to understand. In both cases, Daniel is able to interpret the message that warns the king of an impending disaster in which the Babylonian wise men either are absent or impotent to help. While having a similar plot, these chapters are set in the reigns of two quite different kings, Nebuchadnezzar and Belshazzar, who each bring a different attitude to Daniel and his God.

After exploring the tales of court contest, we then turn our attention in chapters 8 and 9 to the second type of court tale in the first half of the book of Daniel. Here, the ante is raised from contest to conflict. In the first group (the tales of court contest) as we saw in part one, Daniel and/or his three friends can do what the Babylonian wise men were unable to do. Indeed, in the case of understanding Nebuchadnezzar's dream, they actually saved the lives of the pagan wise men.

In Daniel 3 and 6, however, we learn about the animosity of the foreign (Babylonian and Persian) wise men. Daniel and his friends have gained notoriety and authority in the foreign court and the native wise men don't like it. Thus, they try to have them removed from the scene. However, as we will see, God had a different idea in mind.

These two chapters share many similarities but also have differences. Indeed, we will see that the similarities of plot are striking, while the characters are different. In Daniel 3, the three friends have an appearance without Daniel as they encounter conflict in Nebuchadnezzar's court. In Daniel 6, Daniel makes a solo appearance without the three friends as he encounters conflict in Darius's court. In both, however, we again learn that in spite of present difficulties, God is in control, and he will have the final victory.

Having reviewed the stories that compose the first part of the book, we then will turn to chapters 10–12, the last six chapters of Daniel. As noted above, we have an abrupt shift in genre—from court tales, a form of historiographical narration that recounts past events, to apocalyptic visions that use highly figurative language to talk about future events. Interestingly, only the first vision has a short introduction by Daniel (7:1) with a short introduction to Daniel's speech ("Daniel said" [7:2]), and after that the visions are narrated in the first person by Daniel himself.

Though the second half of the book is dramatically different in genre, perspective, and tone, the main message is clearly the same: in spite of present difficulties, God is in control, and he will have the final victory.

The book of Daniel thus has two major parts. The first six chapters are stories about Daniel and his three friends in a foreign court. The next six (at least through 12:4) are four apocalyptic visions. All the stories and the visions hammer away at the main theme: in spite of present difficulties, God is in control, and he will have the final victory.

The book ends, as we will see in chapter 12, with God's agents giving Daniel final instructions concerning how he should behave and think in light of the fact that God is in control and will have the final victory, though that reality is not yet clear. At the moment it looks like evil and powerful people are in control. Once again, the book of Daniel makes it clear that evil will have a certain end and Daniel (and all of us) should act in the light of the certain reality of God's ultimate victory.

FOUR

Forced to Train in
a Hostile Environment

Part 1: Daniel 1

In our survey of the historical background of the book of Daniel, we noted that the book opens with a reference to Nebuchadnezzar's siege of Jerusalem (Dan 1:1-2, 606/05 BC) during the reign of King Jehoiakim of Judah. What the book's narrator tells us that would not be apparent to any human observer is that Nebuchadnezzar's victory was the result of God's efforts. He communicates this important information with the simple phrase, "The Lord delivered Jehoiakim king of Judah into his hand" (Dan 1:2).

BECOMING A VASSAL OF BABYLON (DAN 1:1-4)

Thus, the powerful and rapidly expanding Babylonian Empire under its new energetic ruler Nebuchadnezzar reduces Judah and its capital Jerusalem to the status of a vassal nation. What follows is typical of this particular relationship according to ancient Near Eastern protocol, though there is a slight variation due to the nature of Israel's unique religion.

When a powerful empire like Babylon first subjugated a smaller nation like Judah into the empire, it often did not remove the king or simply incorporate the territory into the empire. Rather, the empire required the lesser state, often referred to as the vassal, to pay annual tribute and serve the interests of the empire. We have a number of ancient treaties, some—the so-called Neo-Assyrian treaties[1]—from approximately a century before the time of Daniel, that are between an emperor and a lesser king that demonstrates that the latter could not have, say, an independent foreign policy as well as other requirements imposed on them. What is interesting when it comes to Daniel 1 is that the actions that are described here are exactly what we would expect from other historical examples from the ancient Near East.

First, we note that Nebuchadnezzar removed "the articles from the temple of God. . . . And put [them] in the treasure house of his god" (Dan 1:2). Typically the conquering king would take the idol representing the chief god of the defeated nation and place it in his own temple. We have many examples, including the much earlier time when Babylon itself was defeated by the Iranian state Elam, which took the statue of Marduk to its capital city only to have the statue be recaptured years later and sent back to Babylon.[2] To a modern reader, this sounds a bit like the child's game capture the flag, but of course the consequences were serious and real. The theology behind this move is either that the god of the defeated nation was himself defeated by the god of the more powerful nation or that the former came over to the side of the more powerful nation due to some failing on the part of his people.

Israel, though, was an aniconic religion; that is, it did not use statues to represent their God. Indeed, the second commandment explicitly forbids the construction of such an idol:

> You shall not make for yourself an image in the form of anything in heaven above or on the earth beneath or in the waters below. You shall not bow down to them or worship them; for I, the LORD your God, am a jealous God, punishing the children for the sin of the parents to the third and fourth generation of those who hate me, but showing love to a thousand generations of those who love me and keep my commandments. (Ex 20:4-6)

That said, one might expect that Nebuchadnezzar would take the Ark of the Covenant, which was housed in the holy of holies and was the most potent symbol of God's presence on earth. Indeed, earlier in Israel's history, during the youth of Samuel, the Philistines captured the ark and placed it in the temple of their chief god Dagan (1 Sam 4:1-11; 5:1-5). The Philistines, however, soon learned that Israel's God Yahweh had neither been defeated nor come over to the side of the Philistines, and they returned the ark to Israel (1 Sam 6).

But by this time the ark no longer existed.³ Accordingly, Nebuchadnezzar took the "articles from the temple" instead and brought them to his temple, presumably the temple of his chief god, Marduk, in Babylon. These articles included all or at least some of the things listed in 1 Kings 7:48-50. But these articles also included "gold and silver goblets" that are not listed in Kings but were likely used for drink offerings at the temple in Jerusalem. These items will make an ominous reappearance in Daniel 5.

Before moving on, we should take note of a subtle point that the narrator of Daniel is making that is easily missed by those who read modern English translations of the story. Daniel 1:2 tells us that Nebuchadnezzar took the articles from the Jerusalem temple to "the temple of his god in Babylonia." As the NIV footnote tells us, the word translated "Babylonia" is the word *Shinar*, not the typical word *Babel*. This rare reference intends to draw our attention back to Genesis 11:2 and the Tower of Babel (here too called "Shinar") story. As Jin Hee Han points out, this connects Nebuchadnezzar's act with "the primeval hubris of the place where humans built the tower of Babel."⁴

"BABYLON UNIVERSITY"

At this time, Nebuchadnezzar issues a second command to Ashpenaz, the "chief of his court officials, to bring into the king's service some of the Israelites from the royal family and the nobility" (Dan 1:3). Here we are introduced to Daniel and his three friends, Hananiah, Mishael, and Azariah.

The taking of members of the young noble class was also typical of the day when a sovereign nation brought a vassal into its control. The sovereign nation would require that the vassal nation send its young noble class to the homeland in order to be trained in their ways in order to serve the interests of the empire. Those interests might entail that the young nobles eventually return to their own country in order to rule in the interests of the empire. We have an example of this strategy reflected in the Amarna Letters written by Canaanite city kings of places like Shechem, Gezer, Lachish, and Jerusalem to their overlord, the Egyptian Pharaoh.[5] These letters come from the fourteenth century BC, much earlier than the time of Daniel, but still they reflect the general practice that we read about in Daniel 1. The young nobles in this case would become attuned to the culture of Egypt, returning to their Canaanite cities, with (the Egyptians hoped) a positive attitude toward Egypt.

Though the purpose was different, the strategy was the same when Nebuchadnezzar had Ashpenaz take young nobles from Jerusalem to Babylon for training. The focus is on Daniel and his three friends, though presumably there could have been even more Judean vassals than these four.

The Babylonian rationale for taking these young men was to train them so that they could serve the interests of Babylon in the core of the empire. Babylon, after all, was a successful empire growing at breakneck speed at the end of the seventh century BC, when Jerusalem became their vassal. One problem with the rapid growth of an empire is that the empire becomes overextended, and then the bureaucracy at the core grows weak. By training Daniel and his friends (and presumably many other vassal nobles), the Babylonians could replenish their homeland administration.

Nebuchadnezzar ordered Ashpenaz to select from the Judeans "young men without any physical defect, handsome, showing aptitude for every kind of learning, well informed, quick to understand, and qualified to serve in the king's palace" (Dan 1:4). We don't know exactly how old Daniel and his friends are at this moment, but the Hebrew term *yeladim*, here translated "young men," would likely indicate someone in their teens or younger. That Daniel was still alive in the third year of Cyrus (ca. 536 BC), almost seventy years after he was taken to Babylon in the first place, also suggests that he was relatively young at this time.

The chosen young men were also to be both physically attractive and intellectually capable. The Babylonian court apparently did not want unattractive smart people or dumb attractive people, but rather people who were pleasant to look at and intelligent enough to contribute to the management of the state. In a moment, though, we will reflect on the question of what struck the Babylonians as good looking and what kind of intelligence they were interested in.

But for now we can see that whatever natural beauty and intellectual capabilities these young men had, Nebuchadnezzar wanted to enhance them by having them trained. Thus, he sends them to what I call "Babylonian University" for three years of education in "the language and literature of the Babylonians" (Dan 1:4).

What do we know about the language and literature of the Babylonians? As it turns out, quite a bit, since over the past century or so we have learned much about Babylonian culture and scribal training through the recovery of ancient cuneiform tablets. What we learn reminds us just how toxic this study would have been to the faith of Daniel and his three friends.

At this time, commonly referred to as the Neo-Babylonian period, Aramaic was the spoken language, but Akkadian was the language of the literature that Daniel and his contemporary scribes would have studied. Akkadian is an extremely difficult language to master, and really only the scribes would have known it.

Daniel and his friends would have learned Akkadian by reading the well-known myths and epics of Mesopotamian culture, for instance the creation epics Enuma Elish and Atrahasis. The latter would have included not only an account of the creation of the cosmos and humanity by their chief god, Marduk, and other pagan deities but also the Babylonian version of the flood.[6] Daniel and his friends would also have read about the flood in the Gilgamesh Epic, but rather than featuring Yahweh, their God, the Babylonian version speaks of Enlil, whose plan to destroy humanity by means of the flood was spoiled by the god Ea, who told Utnapishtim to build an ark so that he, his family, some others, and the animals could survive the flood.

My point here is that the required courses that Daniel and his three friends would have taken extolled gods that they would have considered false gods. These myths and epics would have been blasphemous, attributing creation and flood not to their God Yahweh but rather to others.

But this part of the curriculum pales in significance to the major part of their training—divination. Babylonian wise men would be trained in the techniques of all types of divination. Perhaps the best attested type of divination of the day was the interpretation of the internal organs of sheep, especially the liver. We have extensive literature on this subject as well as clay models of livers that helped diviners understand the significance of the texture, color, and shape of various parts of the organ. The study of the stars—astrology—was yet another means of probing future events, and the list could go on and on.

But for our understanding of the book of Daniel, as we will see as soon as we turn to Daniel 2, we find the practice of dream interpretation in Babylon the most significant. Babylonian dream interpretation operated differently than it did in the Old Testament. In Babylon, dreamers who needed interpretation would tell the interpreter the contents of their dream, and then the diviner would consult dream commentaries in order to determine the meaning.[7]

We will examine the significance of the difference between this mode of interpretation and Daniel's later actions when we take a look at Daniel 2. For now, we are simply interested in the overall training to which Daniel and his friends were subjected. In a word, this training was hostile to their deep faith in Yahweh. It promoted false gods, and it used pagan methods of divination.

But what we should note is that not only did Daniel and his friends not protest this education, they actually were judged the top of their class at the end of their three-year training. Granted, refusal or protest may well have meant death, but we know from later stories that Daniel and his friends would rather die than compromise their faith.

Not only that but these four young men were subjected to other abuses where one might expect that they would protest. When they arrived in Babylon, they had their names changed. Daniel became Belteshazzar, Hananiah became Shadrach, Mishael became Meshach, and Azariah became Abed-Nego. Names are important things even today, but in antiquity they carried even more significance being connected to one's deity. In this case, the young men's Hebrew names, which glorified the true God, were changed to glorify pagan Babylonian gods. We know clearly what the Hebrew names mean, but in a couple cases the Babylonian names are murky to us because the Babylonian names were being transcribed from Hebrew to the language of the Babylonians (Akkadian). But what we can see is as follows:

Daniel, "God is my judge," is changed to Belteshazzar, "the divine lady protects the king."

Hananiah, "Yahweh is gracious to me," is changed to Shadrach, which is unclear.

Mishael, "Who is like God?," is changed to Meshach, which is unclear.

Azariah, "Yahweh is my helper," is changed to Abed-Nego, "the servant of the god Nego" (perhaps a reference to Nabu).

The pattern is clear and typical of a culture that is trying to co-opt another culture. By replacing their names with new ones, the Babylonians were trying to distance these young men from their Israelite and Yahweh-fearing lives to ones that conformed to the Babylonian worldview.

We don't know how Daniel and his friends reacted to this change in their own minds or even among themselves. From everything we learn about their deep faith, we can certainly surmise that they were deeply unhappy about this change. But what we do know is that they did not make any kind of public protest or even display of their unhappiness. They did not feel that this change was something that required them to draw a line in the sand.

Indeed, and this point is a bit speculative, there may have been even a more dramatic change imposed on these men. We began by pointing out that Ashpenaz, who is the official in charge of the young men, is given the title "chief of his court officials" (Dan 1:3). At least that is the way the Hebrew phrase *rav saris* is translated by the NIV and other popular English translations. However, the word *sar* more specifically means "eunuch," and the phrase could be translated easily as something like "chief eunuch." This reminds us of the fact that in ancient Near Eastern courts, many of the king's servants were made eunuchs.

Now there is a debate over whether *sar*, "eunuch," should be taken literally here. Indeed, back in Genesis, Potiphar is a *sar* who was married (Gen 39:1). Perhaps *sar* has become a technical term for a servant in the royal court whether or not that person has actually become a eunuch, or so the argument goes.

However, we should remember what Isaiah told Hezekiah would be a punishment for allowing the Babylonian ruler of his day (about a century before Daniel), Merodach-Baladan, to see the treasures of his kingdom:

> The time will surely come when everything in your palace, and all that your predecessors have stored up until this day, will be carried off to Babylon. Nothing will be left, says the LORD. And some of your descendants, your own flesh and blood who will be born to you, will be taken away, and they will become eunuchs in the palace of the king of Babylon. (Is 39:6-7)

In the light of this passage, it seems likely that we are to understand that Daniel and his friends were made eunuchs as part of their transition to serve in the Babylonian court. And even at this point we don't hear protest.

Diet. Protest comes, though, in reference to Nebuchadnezzar's mandated diet. Surprisingly, the narrator pays significant attention to this issue, thus making it a pivotal issue in the plot. In Daniel 1:5, we read that the king not only required that the young men undergo training as Babylonian wise men but that they eat a diet "of food and wine from the king's table." When Ashpenaz attempted to serve them the food and wine from the king's table, they asked that they not be required to eat it but rather be given water and vegetables. Ashpenaz refused their request because he feared that they would look worse than the other men in the training program (Dan 1:10). Daniel, though, quietly convinced the person who delivered the food to make the substitution. Thus, they successfully avoided the required food.

But why? Why is food so important to Nebuchadnezzar and to Daniel? What is the issue at stake for both of them?

From Ashpenaz's reaction it has to do with physical appearance. He worries that if he allows Daniel and his friends to eat vegetables and to drink water then they will look worse than the others. But, even after a mere ten-day trial, "they looked healthier and better nourished than any of the young men who ate the royal food" (Dan 1:15), and we assume that since at the end of the three years they were judged far superior to their peers that this continued even after three years of their stringent diet.

But again, what is going on?

We can assume that the original readers knew exactly what is going on, but we, twenty-first-century readers, need to put ourselves back in that time and consider the options.

One possibility that springs immediately to mind has to do with the Old Testament food laws (Lev 11). Israelites were only allowed to eat certain types of food, and this diet both differentiated them from Gentiles like Babylonians but also kept them from eating with them. As we consider this possibility, we have to rule it out for a couple of reasons. First, while it is possible, though not clear, that the food might be non-kosher, there was no similar prohibition for the wine. Why water rather than wine if it was a matter of keeping dietary restrictions?

Then, second, if we fast-forward to Daniel 10:3, which takes place much later in time, we see that Daniel was then in the regular habit of eating choice food and meat and drinking wine. We learn his eating habits because he just received a startling vision that took his appetite away. So it appears that whatever Daniel and the friends were doing in chapter 1 only pertains to the three-year training period.

Perhaps their refusal then is more of a political than a religious statement. It is true that eating from the "king's table" (Dan 1:5) indicated a kind of political fealty (see 2 Kings 25:29). Perhaps the four Hebrew men were simply saying, "We refuse to recognize your political authority over us!"

Well, if so, it is a pretty weak protest. First of all, it is totally private. The only person who knows is the delivery man (who probably ate the royal food and drank the wine). And secondly, where would the vegetables come from? Likely, the "king's table" (or supplies).

But this then leads to a third possibility. We know that the royal food was offered to the gods before it was consumed. In a masterful chapter on "The Care and Feeding of the Gods," A. Leo Oppenheim describes how all the food was offered to the gods and whatever they did not eat was then consumed by the royal household.[8]

But again, the problem is that, unlike the New Testament meat that was offered to the gods (see 1 Cor 8:9-13), the Babylonians offered all the food—vegetables included—to the gods. Thus, we are left with a less obvious solution, at least to us. The four Hebrew men ate vegetables and drank water in order to give their God room to work.

First, let's remember that the goal of the food was to make the men look healthy and well nourished. While we might think that meant they were lean and well muscled, the remains of ancient Near Eastern art would lead us in a different direction.

We must remember that male and female beauty standards differ from culture to culture and from time to time. I remember talking to an African student who was studying at the seminary where I was teaching. He missed his wife, and he wistfully and lovingly said, "She is so fat." He then noticed I was a bit mystified by his comment and told me, "You Americans for some reason like thin women. We Africans appreciate a plump woman." For now, I will bracket the question of the appropriateness of having such cultural standards of beauty (which is a modern issue) and simply say that we know the standards of male beauty in Babylon through their art.

When we look at the low reliefs that have been recovered by archaeological investigation of Mesopotamia, we see that men are depicted in one of two ways. The king and the warrior class are indeed bristling with muscles. On the other hand, wise men (like Daniel and his colleagues) are pictured as bald, big eyed (a symbol of intelligence), and chubby. That is the look that Nebuchadnezzar was going for.

Thus, at the end, when Nebuchadnezzar evaluated Daniel and his friends as the top of their class, he would have taken credit through his education and his diet for their intelligence and their looks. However, Daniel and his friends knew (as does the reader) that they were good-looking in the Babylonian sense not because of their royally mandated diet but in spite of it. *God* made them pleasingly plump, *not* the rich food and wine of the king's table.

Though Nebuchadnezzar thinks he is in control, we know that it is God who is in control. And since God is in control, his people have success even when they are in dangerous circumstances. The king found them "ten times better than all the magicians and enchanters in his whole kingdom" (Dan 1:20).

But wait a minute. What does that mean? It means that they can read Akkadian better than anyone else. They have mastered the epics and myths that praise false gods. It means that they can read a liver to discern the future better than anyone else. It means that they are skilled astrologers and that they can interpret dreams by consulting the commentaries. These would be the standards by which Nebuchadnezzar would judge them. They have gone to Babylonian University, and they have become the valedictorians.

Is this wisdom, the wisdom that they learned from "Babylonian University," their true wisdom? We learn the answer to this question when we turn now to Daniel 2, which, though in one sense a separate narrative, is the second part of the story begun in Daniel 1.

DISCUSSION QUESTIONS

1. How did the Babylonians change the lives of Daniel and his three friends?

2. What was the religious significance of the changes?

3. Where did Daniel and his three friends draw the line and refuse to do what the Babylonians asked of them? Why?

4. At the end of Daniel 1, what would Nebuchadnezzar have thought about his control over the lives of Daniel and the three friends? What would Daniel have thought?

FIVE

Forced to Train in a Hostile Environment

Part 2: Daniel 2

I n the opening chapter of the book of Daniel, the Babylonians deport Daniel and his three friends to the city of Babylon, where they are forced to train for service in the royal court. They began with a three-year training that was intended to shape their bodies and minds to Babylonian specifications. In the previous chapter, we observed the extent to which the Babylonian authorities attempted to distance these four men from their own culture and religion and move them toward a Babylonian worldview and lifestyle, which was hostile to their deep faith in Yahweh.

At the end of the training, the king judged them vastly superior to their fellow students. He himself surely would have taken credit for their conformity to the looks expected of Babylonian wise men (chubby) as well as their thinking, particularly in the area of divination. In Daniel 1, the narrator of the book, however, has taken us behind the scenes and shown us that the four men had achieved the proper look not because of Nebuchadnezzar's prescribed diet but in spite of their diet of vegetables and water. That diet should have led to their being thin and wan. But, no, they were more chubby and healthy looking than any of the other trainees. The reader is left with no other conclusion than that God was the one who made them look so appropriate for their position at court.

But then, what about their minds? That was formed by their training in what we are calling Babylonian University, wasn't it? The second story in the book (Dan 2) addresses that question.

Daniel 2 is the first explicit example of what we referred to as a court tale of contest. There was a contest of sorts in chapter one, but it was implicit. We do not hear about the other trainees in Babylonian University, but certainly there were a number of them. When the four men were judged as superior to all the others, that meant they graduated at the top of their class and thus won the contest. But again, since the other students aren't explicitly mentioned, at best the contest is behind the scenes.

In chapter 2, however, the contest is explicit. In the one corner of the rivalry, we have Daniel and his three friends. In the other corner, we have the "magicians, enchanters, sorcerers and astrologers" (Dan 2:2). We should note here that the term *Chaldean* is used in the Hebrew text, and it is translated as "astrologers" (see NIV footnote). *Chaldean* in many contexts is simply an ethnic term since the Chaldeans were an Aramaic-speaking tribe that rose to prominence in southern Mesopotamia—that is, Babylon. Nebuchadnezzar and the ruling party were all Chaldeans. Here, however, Chaldean takes on a specialized sense. The practice of astrology was closely aligned with this particular group, so the term *Chaldean* came to be used for "astrologer." For our purposes, it highlights the fact that this contest, while primarily a contest between the true God and false gods, is also a contest between Babylon and Judah.

NEBUCHADNEZZAR ASKS FOR THE CONTENT OF HIS DREAM

At first, Daniel and his friends are not even on the scene. The plot thickens when King Nebuchadnezzar has a disturbing dream. At first, he follows typical Babylonian protocol and summons the "magicians, enchanters, sorcerers and astrologers." But then he radically departs from that protocol when he not only asks him to interpret the dream but also to tell him the contents of the dream.

We should remember what we said in the previous chapter. Babylonian dream interpretation begins with the dreamer telling the interpreter the content of a dream and then the interpreter goes to the dream commentaries and researches its meaning. These Babylonian wise men have made no claim to be able to tell the king what he dreamed. And they react accordingly. "May the king live forever! Tell your servants the dream, and we will interpret it" (Dan 2:4).

The king unexpectedly grows angry and demands that they tell him the contents of the dream or he will have them "cut into pieces" and have their houses "turned into piles of rubble" (Dan 2:5). On the other hand, he offers them great rewards for successfully completing the task. But, again, the interpreters ask for the contents of the dream (Dan 2:7), and the king grows even more angry, this time believing that they are trying to change his mind.

We do not know why the king makes this unprecedented demand, but the Babylonian wise men make it clear that, according to the Babylonian worldview, what he asks is simply impossible: "There is no one on earth who can do what the king asks! No king, however great and mighty, has ever asked such a thing of any magician or enchanter or astrologer. What the king asks is too difficult. No one can reveal it to the king except the gods, and they do not live among humans" (Dan 2:10-11).

The gauntlet has been thrown down. No human can do what the king asks. Only the gods, and they are inaccessible.

When the wisdom teachers fail to tell him his dream, the king responds by following through on his threat and ordering his guard to put all the wise men to death. This brings Arioch, the commander of his guard, to the door of Daniel and his friends. When Arioch arrived at Daniel's doorstep to put them to death, Daniel responds with patience and politeness, showing himself to be the epitome of a wise man ("Patience brings much competence, but impatience promotes stupidity,"[1] Prov 14:29; see also 16:32 and 25:15). He does not panic but asks for time, which Arioch grants him.

Daniel turns to God, not Babylon, for the interpretation. Daniel knows that the Babylonian wise men were correct to say that no human being could possibly know what the king dreamed or even have a definitive interpretation of that dream. So Daniel, rather than relying on his training in dream interpretation at Babylonian University, turns to the only person who can tell him the dream: God. The four men spend the night praying to God, and God responds by revealing to them the dream and its interpretation. True wisdom comes from God, and those who, like Daniel and his three friends, fear God and turn to him will be wise themselves (Prov 1:7).

God thus answered their prayer and saved them from death. He had revealed to them the contents of Nebuchadnezzar's dream and its interpretation. There was no need for them to consult the dream interpretation books. The first thing Daniel did was praise God:

> Praise be to the name of God for ever and ever;
>> wisdom and power are his.
> He changes times and seasons;
>> he deposes kings and raises up others.
> He gives wisdom to the wise
>> and knowledge to the discerning.
> He reveals deep and hidden things;
>> he knows what lies in darkness,
>> and light dwells with him.
> I thank and praise you, God of my ancestors:
>> You have given me wisdom and power,
> you have made known to me what we asked of you,
>> you have made known to us the dream of the king.
>> (Dan 2:20-23)

God had just given them knowledge of the contents of the king's dream and also the ability to interpret it. Thus, they praise God's wisdom and his power. Their willingness to go to God to get the answers to their questions shows that they fear God and look to him for wisdom; they are not "wise in their own eyes" (Prov 26:5, 12, 16; 28:11).

Yahweh's wisdom is superior. Before going on to the interpretation of Nebuchadnezzar's dream, let's pause here and reflect on the contrast between Babylonian wisdom and God's wisdom. Many readers of Daniel 2 go right to the fantastic dream and its interpretation and believe that the first part of the chapter is simply setting the scene for the dream itself. Actually, though, the main point of the book is not the dream but rather showing the superiority of Yahweh's wisdom to anything that the four men might have learned back at Babylonian University.

True wisdom comes directly from Yahweh, who gives it to those who fear him. At the end of chapter 1, we saw that Daniel and his friends were judged as superior in mind and body to the other students. The Babylonians attributed their success to their training and diet, but the four men (and those who read chapter 1) knew that their good looks came about in spite of their diet. By eating vegetables and drinking water, they gave God room to work. But when it came to their minds, they were judged as superior based on their mastery of the Babylonian curriculum. Here in chapter two, we learn that "wisdom" gets them nowhere. They had to depend on God and turn to him in faithful prayer to receive the answers to their questions.

In this, Daniel and his friends illustrate the type of wisdom presented in the book of Proverbs, where we learn that "the fear of the LORD is the beginning of knowledge" (Prov 1:7). Job is yet another example of this type of fear: Job at the end simply submits himself to God in the midst of his suffering and in an anticipation of his final conclusion he announces, "The fear of the Lord—that is wisdom" (Job 28:28). And finally we remember the conclusion of the book of Ecclesiastes. "Now all has been heard; here is the conclusion of the matter: fear God and keep his commandments" (Eccles 12:13). These three wisdom books all agree, along with Daniel, that true wisdom comes only from God and is accessed only through having a proper relationship with him.[2]

THE DREAM AND ITS INTERPRETATION (DAN 2:24-49)

We may read quickly over it, but we shouldn't. Notice what Daniel says first to Arioch: "Do not execute the wise men of Babylon" (Dan 2:24). We should take note that Daniel shows concern for these pagan wise men, some of whose members will later seek to have him killed.

In the history of interpretation there have been those who have criticized Daniel for this. Calvin said Daniel made a mistake here by not waiting until all the pagan wise men are killed,[3] but we should see here an example of how even during the Old Testament time period, God's chosen people bring benefit to those outside the covenant in a way anticipated by God's promise to Abraham: "All peoples on earth will be blessed through you" (Gen 12:3).

We should also observe how Arioch introduces Daniel when he takes him to Nebuchadnezzar. He does not call him by his personal name—neither Daniel nor Belteshazzar—but rather as "a man among the exiles from Judah" (Dan 2:25). Even here, before he answers Nebuchadnezzar's question, there is a reminder that, on the surface of things at least, Babylon is in control. Daniel is an exile. Still Nebuchadnezzar asks if he can tell him the contents of his dream and its interpretation. Daniel's response to this question is significant. He agrees with the earlier statement of the Babylonian wise men when he admits, "No wise man, enchanter, magician or diviner can explain to the king the mystery he has asked about" (Dan 2:27). The Babylonian wise men went on to say that only the gods could tell the king the contents of the dream but that the gods don't "live among humans" (Dan 2:11). Here is where Daniel disagrees when he says, "There is a God in heaven who reveals mysteries. He has shown King Nebuchadnezzar what will happen in days to come" (Dan 2:28).

We thus encounter the first of a series of visions, but the only one that appears in the first half of the book. We will see, though, that its message will be very similar to the vision in Daniel 7. We will reflect on those similarities when we come to that chapter.

The dream. We begin, as Daniel does, with a description of the dream itself (Dan 2:31-35). At the center of the dream is "an enormous, dazzling statue, awesome in appearance" (Dan 2:31). What is particularly striking about the statue is that it is composed of many different metals. Daniel first describes the head of gold, then the chest and arms of silver, the belly and thighs of bronze, and the legs of iron. He concludes by mentioning the feet, which are not totally metallic but a mixture of iron and baked clay.

The description then shifts to a rock cutout, presumably from a cliff face or a mountainside. Daniel makes a point of saying that the cutting out of the rock was not done "by human hands" (Dan 2:34). This rock then hit the fragile feet of the statue, causing the whole thing to disintegrate and be blown away by the wind "like chaff" (Dan 2:35). The rock not only survives the collision, but then it becomes a huge mountain that fills the earth.

Knowing the contents of the dream was even more amazing than being able to interpret it. That is likely why Nebuchadnezzar insisted that an interpreter tell him what he dreamed before interpreting it.[4] Anyone can take a stab at interpreting the significance of a dream, but only someone who has a relationship with the divine realm could inform him of his dream. Thus Nebuchadnezzar, convinced that Daniel has learned what he dreamed from the divine realm, is ready to hear its interpretation.

The statue and the kingdoms. The statue, it appears, represents various kingdoms; each part of the statue—from head to toes—are kingdoms that succeed each other. Only the first kingdom is identified, and it is Nebuchadnezzar's Babylon. He is the head of gold. Daniel interestingly acknowledges that Nebuchadnezzar is king of kings and has great power and sway over God's creation, human and animal (Dan 2:38).

The silver, bronze, iron, and iron/clay kingdoms are not identified. After all, these are future kingdoms from Daniel's perspective. Still there are certain attributes or qualifiers associated with each of them. The second kingdom is said to be "inferior" to Nebuchadnezzar's Babylon (Dan 2:39), presumably like silver is less valuable than gold.

The third kingdom, though, is said to "rule over the whole earth" (Dan 2:39). Note that the vast extent of its rule does not necessarily mean that its reach extends beyond that of Babylon, whose reach was also said to be worldwide. The fact that this third kingdom is represented by bronze probably indicates that, though it has far-reaching dominion, it too is inferior to the previous since bronze is less valuable than silver and gold, though this is not made explicit.

If the bronze kingdom is less valuable than the previous two, the "iron" kingdom is even more so. But though iron may be less expensive, it is also much stronger certainly than bronze. Iron weapons are more lethal than bronze weapons, and so not surprisingly this fourth kingdom "breaks and smashes everything—and as iron breaks things to pieces, so it will crush and break all the others" (Dan 2:40).

The final focus is on the feet made of clay and iron. The fact that half the ingredients are iron may indicate an extension of the fourth kingdom. But the mixture with clay points out the divided nature of this kingdom. The clay also introduces fragility to the feet that we will see provides a point of vulnerability to this statue.

So we note, along with Nebuchadnezzar, that the interpretation of his dream indicates a succession of kingdoms, but again only the first kingdom is identified with a specific kingdom—namely, Babylon. While only the second kingdom is explicitly said to be inferior to the first, the decreasing value of the metals that follow implies that in some sense at least the following kingdoms are inferior to those that preceded it.

Interpretation. As many people know, interpreters over the centuries have tried to extend the interpretation beyond that given to Daniel by God. From a later historical perspective, we are able to see how history developed with one world power surpassing another. Indeed, scholarly focus has, in my opinion, wrongly concentrated on trying to identify the various kingdoms. As we will see, this attempt to identify them has led to disagreements and heated debate (see on the four kingdoms in Daniel 7, chapter 10). But, while not totally inappropriate, this interpretive move takes our eyes off the main message of the vision.

It does not really matter which kingdoms are represented by these metals; they represent successive world powers that dominate the people of God beginning with Babylon. The main message of the dream comes with the next episode after the description of the statue.

From the statue our attention is diverted to the rock cut out of a cliff or mountainside. The observation that this was done "not by human hands" subtly indicates that God did it. This rock then smashed the fragile feet of the statue (Dan 2:34), and as a result the whole statue came crumbling down. This rock too represents a kingdom, this one set up by God. God will destroy the nations that oppress his people and replace it with his kingdom that will fill the whole earth (Dan 2:35).

Daniel's God-given ability to describe and then interpret Nebuchadnezzar's dream leads Nebuchadnezzar to honor Daniel and to praise his God (Dan 2:46-47). He also promoted Daniel to a high position and at Daniel's request also gave his three friends high positions.

CONCLUSION

We identified Daniel 2 as a tale of court contest. The contest was over who could provide not only the interpretation but also the content of Nebuchadnezzar's dream. The Babylonian wise men were unable to do it, but thanks to God, Daniel could provide the king with what he wanted to know. Daniel and his three friends were threatened with death (in spite of present difficulties), but God revealed to them the mystery (God is in control) and their lives were spared (and he will have the final victory). The dream itself indicated that the world was and will be dominated by powerful human kingdoms that do damage, particularly to the people of God (in spite of present difficulties), but that God will eventually bring those kingdoms to an end (God is in control), and he will establish his own kingdom to fill the world (and he will have the final victory).

Finally, we have seen that Daniel 1 and 2 have a close relationship that together show that, though Nebuchadnezzar has tried to assert his control over the four young Judean men, God is the one who gives them what they need. Their bodies are well nourished not because of Nebuchadnezzar's diet but because God made them that way in spite of the fact that they were eating vegetables and drinking water. They were wise not because of their graduation from Babylonian University but because God revealed his wisdom to them.

We move next to Daniel 4. Here Nebuchadnezzar has another dream that Daniel must interpret.

DISCUSSION QUESTIONS

1. Why do you think Nebuchadnezzar insisted that the wisdom teachers tell him the contents of his dream before they interpreted it?

2. How did Daniel respond to the situation with wisdom? What lessons can we learn for our own lives from his reactions in this chapter?

3. How does the main theme of the book of Daniel (in spite of present circumstances, God is in control and will have the final victory) work out in this chapter?

4. How does the secondary theme of the book of Daniel (you can not only survive but thrive under oppression) work out in this chapter?

SIX

God Humbles Powerful Nebuchadnezzar

Daniel 4

D aniel 4 begins with a royal proclamation:

King Nebuchadnezzar,

To the nations and peoples of every language, who live in all the earth:

May you prosper greatly!

It is my pleasure to tell you about the miraculous signs and wonders that the Most High God has performed for me.

How great are his signs,
   how mighty his wonders!
His kingdom is an eternal kingdom;
   his dominion endures from generation to generation.
   (4:1-3)

From this point, the king then tells the story that led him to this unbridled praise of Daniel's God.

We should first note a unique feature of this particular chapter. Though we will see that it is a tale of court contest like Daniel 2 (and 5), this chapter is the only one narrated by a character, and that character is none other than the Babylonian king Nebuchadnezzar. We should pause to appreciate this particular shape of the narrative from the perspective of faithful Jewish readers who were living under the oppressive reign of a pagan king, whether Babylonian, Persian, Greek, Roman, or others. Here we have the pagan king who subjugated Jerusalem praising their God. What a reminder that, though matters on the ground look otherwise, God is really in control.

After his astonishing tribute to the true God, Nebuchadnezzar then continues by recounting the course of events that has led to his praise of Yahweh. We know the story is going to end well for Nebuchadnezzar, but we are intrigued by this remarkable opening to know exactly what led to the king's acknowledgment of Yahweh.

At a time when he was at home in Babylon and flourishing, Nebuchadnezzar informs the reader that he had a dream that disturbed his equilibrium. Accordingly, he called his "magicians, enchanters, astrologers and diviners" (Dan 4:7) to help him understand the significance of the dream. Unlike the situation in Daniel 2, the king tells them the contents of his dream, but even so they are unable to interpret it for him, for reasons not given in the story. This time, however, Nebuchadnezzar does not threaten them or even concern himself with them again. Rather, he calls Daniel in order to tell him the dream.

We should note that Nebuchadnezzar makes a point of his new name, Belteshazzar, and notes explicitly that the name embeds the name of his—that is, Nebuchadnezzar's—god. He further goes on to say that "the spirit of the holy gods is in him" (Dan 4:8). Though some overzealous readers of the book of Daniel would say that Nebuchadnezzar becomes a worshiper of the true God through Daniel's witness, it is much more likely that Nebuchadnezzar remained a polytheist through to the end, but the amazing development is that he does indeed acknowledge not only that Yahweh is one of those gods but a more important one than perhaps he thought at first.

Rather than worrying about discerning Nebuchadnezzar's exact spiritual state, we should ask what purpose his positive attitude toward

Yahweh served in the book. Again, for a Jew who is being oppressed by a foreign power, Yahweh can manifest himself in such a way that even arrogant powerful rulers such as Nebuchadnezzar must acknowledge his supremacy.

THE DREAM RECOUNTED

The king then informed Daniel, identified as "chief of the magicians" and possessor of "the spirit of the holy gods" (Dan 4:9), of the content of the dream. The focus is on a large tree in the middle of the earth that grew so big that its top touched the sky and its branches extended to all the earth. This tree bore fruit that was used to feed all the creatures of the earth and to provide shelter to them as well. But then a "holy one, a messenger" (Dan 4:13) arrived on the scene. The word translated "messenger" by the NIV is actually, as the footnote to the translation indicates, a "watchman." This language is used of angels.

This angel then called for the destruction of the tree by cutting it down, stripping its leaves, and scattering its fruit, so the animals and other creatures no longer found protection or sustenance from it. All that was left was a stump and roots, but around the stump the angel ordered an iron and bronze band, presumably so it could not grow again.

At this point, the language changes from describing the fate of the tree to a person, unnamed, referred to simply as "he." This person will be exposed to the elements and will become animal-like himself. Specifically, his mind will become like the mind of an animal. This fate will last for "seven times" or possibly "seven years" (Dan 4:16; see NIV footnote). Whether times or years, the number seven is symbolic and indicates a very long time.

The angels not only describe the fate of the tree and the person whom the tree represents but also the purpose of the destruction of the tree. It is "so that the living may know that the Most High is sovereign over all kingdoms on earth and gives them to anyone he wishes and sets over them the lowliest of people" (Dan 4:17).

After recounting the dream, the king then calls on Daniel to interpret it for him. Daniel himself was perplexed and frightened by the dream, though it is unclear whether he is being empathetic toward the king or worried that the message might bring the king's wrath on him. But after Nebuchadnezzar reassures him, Daniel proceeds with the interpretation.

THE DREAM INTERPRETED

After Nebuchadnezzar's encouragement, Daniel initiates the interpretation. Unlike Daniel 2, we have no mention of Daniel praying to God or an explicit statement that God revealed the interpretation to him. That said, we should remember that Nebuchadnezzar begins the chapter by praising God, who has performed "miraculous signs and wonders" (Dan 4:2). Of course, these signs and wonders also include the events that follow but also, I would argue, the interpretation. Surely Daniel did not have the ability to interpret the dream on his own.

Before Daniel informs the king of the dream's interpretation, he tells him that he wished that the dream applied to the king's enemies rather than to him, perhaps supporting the idea that Daniel is empathetic toward this ruler but perhaps just protecting himself from backlash.

He begins by telling the king that he himself is the large and growing tree. Nebuchadnezzar's kingdom has expanded to the point that it, in effect, covered the whole known world, or at least that part of the world that was considered its core. We know that Babylon under Nebuchadnezzar stretched from the Tigris to the border of Egypt. While reckoning with hyperbole, there is no doubt but that Nebuchadnezzar reigned over the most powerful by far empire ever known to humanity up to this time in history.

But even so, it appears that the prosperity of the king would not last. The angel's decree to cut down the tree anticipates the time when the king's mind would be reduced to an animal-like state and he would live an animal-like existence. He will live in this state for a long period of time ("seven times will pass by for you"; Dan 4:25). He would be animal-like until he acknowledged "that the Most High is sovereign over all kingdoms on earth and gives them to anyone he wishes" (Dan 4:25). Daniel takes this as a warning, not as an unconditional prediction. He urges Nebuchadnezzar to renounce his sin and be kind to the oppressed. If he does, then he can avoid this horrible fate. But it was not to be.

NEBUCHADNEZZAR'S PRIDE

We have commented above about how Daniel 4 is unique in the book by being Nebuchadnezzar's first-person account of events. But we see the narrator intervening briefly in Daniel 4:19 to introduce Nebuchadnezzar's speech to Daniel (called Belteshazzar), but now in Daniel 4:28-33 the narrator takes full control of the story to recount the fulfillment of the dream.

The narrator reports that "all this happened to King Nebuchadnezzar" (Dan 4:28). Perhaps the narrator takes over because, after all, the plot turns to the king's madness. In a sense, he is mentally blanked out until his sanity is restored.

In any case, we hear that a year after his dream, Nebuchadnezzar was on the roof of his palace and looking at Babylon, the magnificent city that he has built. Of course, Nebuchadnezzar did not build Babylon as a new city. Indeed, Babylon far preceded the life of Nebuchadnezzar, extending back at least two millennia before his birth. But Nebuchadnezzar had restored, enlarged, and magnified the city so that it was indeed a symbol of power and wealth. It extended to two thousand acres, enormous by ancient standards. Its walls (with moat), ziggurat, and buildings were the marvel of the ancient world as noted by early Greek historians like Herodotus. The Ishtar Gate that provided entry into the city was a multicolored gem, and its famed Hanging Gardens, built to look like a verdant mountain for Nebuchadnezzar's foreign wife who came from a mountainous region, was considered one of the seven wonders of the ancient world.

While surveying this magnificent scene, Nebuchadnezzar said to himself, "Is not this the great Babylon I have built as the royal residence, by my mighty power and for the glory of my majesty?" (Dan 4:30). This rhetorical question exposed the king's immense pride. From the consequences, we can also say that this assertion of self-importance was a challenge to God's sovereignty. He had been warned, and now God would make an example of him.

Accordingly, this king, the most powerful human being in the world at this time—certainly in the world known to the biblical author—was reduced to beast-like status. This human being who perhaps presumed to be god-like was now like an animal: "He was driven away from people and ate grass like the ox. His body was drenched with the dew of heaven until his hair grew like the feathers of an eagle and his nails like the claws of a bird" (Dan 4:33).

Many have tried to diagnose his malady in order to put a modern medical label on it. The most common diagnosis is boanthropy, the condition of thinking and acting like an ox or a cow. Doing such a diagnosis is extremely speculative and unnecessary. Whether or not we can successfully name the mental disorder, the purpose is clear: this proud king was reduced to being like an animal in order to remember that he is not divine but human.

Thus, while the sickness was severe, the prescription for health was as easy as raising his eyes toward heaven. That was as much as he could do, but that simple gesture communicated that he at last acknowledged the sovereignty of God. God thus restored his sanity, and Nebuchadnezzar, once his mental faculties were restored, praised him:

> His dominion is an eternal dominion;
>> his kingdom endures from generation to generation.
> All the peoples of the earth
>> are regarded as nothing.
> He does as he pleases
>> with the powers of heaven
>> and the peoples of the earth.
> No one can hold back his hand
>> or say to him: "What have you done?" (Dan 4:34-35)

CONCLUSION

What is the purpose of this story? Again, we learn that, though God's people live under the thumb of Babylon (in spite of present difficulties), God can reduce even its very powerful king to the status of an animal (God is in control), and that king when restored will praise him (God will have the final victory). God's presence with his people even in their suffering means that they can not only survive but thrive because Daniel, and not the Babylonian wise men, is able to interpret the king's dream.

And then, finally, we note the theme of pride. God's treatment of Nebuchadnezzar is a warning to all of us who are tempted to pride. This lesson is driven home by the very last sentence of the chapter: "And those who walk in pride he [God] is able to humble" (Dan 4:37).

DISCUSSION QUESTIONS

1. Why does Nebuchadnezzar praise God? Does this necessarily mean that Nebuchadnezzar has become a worshiper of the true God?

2. Why do you think Daniel was afraid to interpret the king's dream in the first place?

3. How does this chapter glorify God? What effect should this have on the ancient reader? On you as a reader today?

4. Summarize how this story reinforces the main theme of the book of Daniel.

SEVEN

Who Can Interpret the Writing on the Wall?

Daniel 5

T he writing is on the wall!" Today we make this announcement when we believe that all indications make it certain that some negative consequence is about to occur. The expression comes from the story in Daniel 5, and we will see that, when the writing appears on the wall, the message is anything but clear at first. Indeed, the writing on the wall becomes yet another occasion for what we are calling a tale of court contest. In this way, Daniel 5 is similar yet different from Daniel 1, 2, and 4. Indeed, there is an especially close relationship with the story found in Daniel 4, and so we will be on the lookout not only for similarities but also for differences between the two.

BELSHAZZAR'S PARTY (DAN 5:1-4)

When we start reading this chapter, we see that there is a new king ruling in Babylon—Belshazzar. Unlike Daniel 4 where Nebuchadnezzar himself is the main narrator of the story, here Belshazzar is a character of the story, and a rather unlikeable one at that, particularly in contrast to Nebuchadnezzar in the earlier story.

For the interesting historical issues surrounding Belshazzar, see chapter two of the present book. For now, just remember that as we find out from Babylonian sources, he is the son of Nabonidus, who is the titular king of Babylon but ruling from an oasis named Tayma in what today is Saudi Arabia. However, since this is the eve of Babylon's destruction, we know from ancient sources outside the Bible that Nabonidus was out in the field leading the Babylonian army against the incursion of Cyrus, king of Persia.[1] He engaged Cyrus near a city called Opis that was some fifty miles north of Babylon. It is possible that this battle had already taken place and that the Babylonian army under Nabonidus had already been defeated, which would have made the city of Babylon vulnerable to Cyrus's army.

Belshazzar, now coregent with his father, was holding the fort back in the city of Babylon, likely aware of his dire situation. It is with this background that we should read the story of his party.

We do have examples of ancient Near Eastern kings throwing banquets on the eve of a battle as a way of rallying leaders to build up their confidence for the coming conflict. Reading Esther 1, for example, in the light of comments by the Greek historian Herodotus helps us realize that Xerxes's lavish banquet was just such a pep rally before he set out on a campaign against the Greeks.[2]

If Belshazzar's party was thrown as the Persian armies, after defeating the rest of the known world at the time, were bearing down on Babylon, we can imagine that Belshazzar was already on edge, perhaps helping to explain the heavy drinking. But his call for the "gold goblets that had been taken from the temple of God in Jerusalem" (Dan 5:3) would have taken on even more significance in light of the impending threat.

This act would have been an attempt, feeble perhaps, at trying to bolster their confidence by remembering Nebuchadnezzar's victory over another nation and its god.[3] The king led the participants of the party in using these sacred goblets for profane purposes as they toasted their own pagan gods. Interestingly, the narrator describes these false gods worshiped by the Babylonians as "gods of gold and silver, of bronze, iron, wood and stone" (Dan 5:4), reminding us that they were idol worshipers.

The golden cups from which Belshazzar and the others were drinking were part of the temple ritual that was used to praise the true and living God, but here they are being used to praise gods made of the same or even inferior materials to the goblets themselves. We are reminded of the type of ridicule that the prophets Isaiah (Is 44:6-23) and Jeremiah (Jer 10:1-10) heaped on the practice of worshiping lifeless idols.

THE FAILED ATTEMPT TO READ THE WRITING ON THE WALL (DAN 5:5-9)

In the midst of what was probably a nervous and forced frivolity, a human hand appeared and started writing on the plaster walls of the palace. Whatever false confidence Belshazzar was manufacturing immediately dissolved, and he reacted with fear when the hand appeared. His fear is described in physical terms by the narrator, "His face turned pale and he was so frightened that his legs became weak and his knees were knocking" (Dan 5:6).[4] Apparently, there was something ominous about this writing even without its interpretation.

Like Nebuchadnezzar in Daniel 2 and 4, Belshazzar starts by calling in the "wise men of Babylon" (Dan 5:7). He does not threaten them as Nebuchadnezzar did in Daniel 2; rather, he promises reward. If one of the wise men can interpret the writing, then that person "will be clothed in purple and have a gold chain placed around his neck, and he will be made the third highest ruler in the kingdom" (Dan 5:7). The gold chain indicates authority of some sort; the purple garment points toward royal authority. The idea of third highest ruler is a bit opaque until we remember, thanks to our extrabiblical sources, that Nabonidus and Belshazzar were one and two.[5]

But, as we saw in the previous tales of court contest, the Babylonian wise men are painfully inadequate for the task. They are unable to interpret the message.

THE QUEEN MOTHER'S CALL FOR DANIEL (DAN 5:10-12)

At this moment, the queen came into the room. She tells the king about Daniel, about whom Belshazzar appears unaware. Questions surround the exact identity of this "queen." We don't know much about Belshazzar besides what we read in the book of Daniel, but this queen addresses him with such authority that it seems likely and widely accepted that this is the queen mother. Queen mothers were known to wield significant authority at times in ancient Near Eastern courts.

Whoever she is, wife or mother, she immediately tries to calm Belshazzar down by giving him an alternative route to an understanding of the writing on the wall. She tells him about Daniel.

She informs him about Daniel's role in his predecessor Nebuchadnezzar's life as the one who was able to interpret dreams and visions for the king. Over the past two decades since the death of Nebuchadnezzar (562 BC) Daniel had for some reason slipped from most royal memory, but the queen (mother) remembers and tells Belshazzar to call him to come and interpret the writing on the wall.

Thus, Belshazzar calls Daniel into his presence. We should notice how he addresses Daniel as "one of the exiles my father the king brought from Judah" (Dan 5:13). Not only does his lack of knowledge of Daniel show disrespect, his reference to him as an exile is demeaning. He goes on to tell him that he has heard of his reputation as a person who has "insight, intelligence and outstanding wisdom" and as someone who has the "spirit of the gods" in him (Dan 5:14). Now he calls on him to demonstrate this ability. He tells him that the Babylonian wise men failed, but that if he is successful he will gain the same rewards that he promised to the Babylonian wise men.

Daniel meets Belshazzar's request with disdain. He has no love or respect for this king, and so he refuses the reward. He also compares him with Nebuchadnezzar in a way that puts Belshazzar in a very bad light.

Nebuchadnezzar was a powerful world ruler. Interestingly, and in keeping with the book's theme that God is in charge, he says that his power was God's gift. God gave him "sovereignty and greatness and glory and splendor" (Dan 5:18). Daniel tells him about the episode in Nebuchadnezzar's life recounted in Daniel 4 when Nebuchadnezzar's pride got to him and God reduced him to an animal-like status to remind him that God, not he, was sovereign.

Nebuchadnezzar humbled himself before God, but Belshazzar did not, just the opposite! Rather than honoring God, he blasphemed him by using the temple goblets to praise false gods. Thus, God "sent the hand that wrote the inscription" (Dan 5:24). Daniel appears only too happy to interpret the ominous message of the writing for this prideful king.

He begins by reading it: MENE, MENE, TEKEL, PARSIN

Here are three different words, the first repeated twice, perhaps for emphasis. He then provides an interpretation, and it turns out that the words are related to Hebrew/Semitic verbs.

MENE comes from a verb that means "to count" or "to number," and according to Daniel's interpretation, "God has numbered the days of your reign and brought it to an end" (Dan 5:26).

TEKEL comes from a verb that means "to weigh" and here is taken in the sense of "evaluation": "You have been weighed on the scales and found wanting" (Dan 5:27).

PERES comes from a verb that means "to divide" and is taken here to mean that Belshazzar's Babylon will be split and given to two Iranian powers, the Medes and the Persians, who have been brought together under Cyrus the Great's leadership.

As the NIV footnote also indicates there may be a double-entendre here since these three words can also be taken as nouns that refer to money: mina, shekel, and a half, moving from more expensive to less, showing perhaps the diminished power of Babylon.

Al Wolters suggests that there is even a triple-entendre. He begins by saying that the reason why the Babylonian wise men had difficulty was not only because the message was in Hebrew but it was unvocalized (no vowels) and without spaces: *mn'tqlprs*. Thus, it could be read according to the two ways described above or, according to Wolters, it could also be understood in a third way with a different vocalization (*menah, tiqqal, paras*) and translated as a sentence: "He has paid out, you are too light, Persia!" Thus again using the metaphor of a scale to indicate God's judgment that is about to come down on Babylon.[6]

After that, the story comes to a sudden conclusion. In spite of Daniel's earlier refusal, Daniel receives the reward. He was "clothed in purple, a gold chain was placed around his neck, and he was proclaimed the third highest ruler in the kingdom" (Dan 5:29). Noting this, the narrator communicates that Daniel was able to do what the Babylonian wise men were unable to do, successfully interpret the writing on the wall.

As a practical matter, however, his promotion was certainly short-lived. That night the doom portended by the writing came true. Belshazzar died by means unspecified, and Darius the Mede, either another name for or a subordinate of Cyrus, took over the kingdom.[7]

CONCLUSION

Thus, again, we learn that in spite of present difficulties, God is in control, and he will have the final victory. The chapter starts with an arrogant Babylonian king blaspheming God and worshipping false gods. The story ends though, with God's agent Daniel, successfully interpreting the writing on the wall that announces the destruction of that king's power.

DISCUSSION QUESTIONS

1. Describe Belshazzar's personality based on his speech and actions. What words would you use to describe him?

2. Why is Daniel so upset with Belshazzar?

3. In your own words, how does this chapter illustrate the main theme (in spite of present circumstances, God is in control and will have the final victory)?

4. In your own words, how does this chapter illustrate the second theme (not only can you survive, you can thrive under oppression)?

EIGHT

The Three Friends and the Fiery Furnace

Daniel 3

U p till now, the three friends of Daniel have had a supporting role in the plot of Daniel. Daniel 3 is the only chapter where they take center stage, appearing without Daniel. Indeed, they don't appear again in the plot after this chapter since Daniel alone appears in Daniel 4–6.

When they were forcibly brought to Babylon as political hostages (Dan 1), they had good Hebrew names (Hananiah, Mishael, and Azariah) that celebrated the God whom they worshiped. They were then given Babylonian names (Shadrach, Meshach, and Abed-Nego) as part of the attempt to reprogram them to serve the interests of the Babylonian Empire (see chapter 4 and comments on Dan 1). In this chapter, the Babylonians consistently use their Babylonian names, which praise pagan deities, and the narrator follows suit. Even so, we will see that these three Jewish men remain steadfast to their faith in Yahweh even in the face of death.

THE GOLDEN STATUE (DAN 3:1-7)

The chapter begins by telling the reader that King Nebuchadnezzar constructed a very large statue on the plain of Dura in Babylon. His intention was to make sure that all the leaders of Babylon would bow before this statue at its dedication. Much about this statue and the motivation behind it remains ambiguous.

First, the size of the statue is odd. Converting cubits into feet, the statue is described as ninety feet (sixty cubits) tall, but only nine feet (six cubits) wide. That would be a pretty tall and a pretty thin statue! Some speculate that the ninety feet includes a pedestal, but we don't know for sure. The height, with or without a pedestal, would allow the statue to be seen by the large crowd of leaders assembled by the king.

More mystifying is the question of what or who the statue represented. The narrator never answers this question, and in one sense it is not important. Perhaps the statue is an idol of a god, but which one? Perhaps Marduk, the chief god of the Babylonian pantheon, or perhaps more likely, the statue could be representing Nebuchadnezzar himself.

After all, we might remember that Daniel had just interpreted his dream that featured a multimetaled statue where Nebuchadnezzar was the head of gold. That surely would have pleased Nebuchadnezzar, but perhaps he worried because the dream also foretold that his golden kingdom would be replaced by another. Perhaps making a statue of himself that was golden from head to foot was a way to resist the implicit message that he and his kingdom were finite.

Whether god or king the statue represents a loyalty test. Would all of his leaders bow to the statue? If they did not, then, in the mind of Nebuchadnezzar at least, they would represent a threat to his empire.

Lists. Before moving on to the next episode of the story, we should note the use of long, repeated lists in this chapter, beginning in this section. In the first place, the leaders themselves are enumerated as "the satraps, prefects, governors, advisers, treasurers, judges, magistrates and all the other provincial officials" (Dan 3:2, 3, 27). In the second place, the bowing was announced and accompanied by music from a band that included "the horn, flute, zither, lyre, harp, pipe and all kinds of music" (Dan 3:5, 7, 10, 15). Finally, while it is the leaders who are assembled, they seem to represent the "nations and peoples of every language" throughout the kingdom, and that is yet another repeated, though shorter, list (Dan 3:4, 7, 29).

Why are these long lists repeated regularly in the chapter when a simple pronoun might do? Well, the effect is that the whole event seems forced, stilted, pretentious, and perhaps comical. It makes Nebuchadnezzar look controlling and insecure.

The music starts, and the people bow. At first sight, it looks as if everyone complies with the order. But then news arrives of a small group of "Jews" who did not bow, and the action really starts.

THE THREE FRIENDS CONFRONTED (DAN 3:8-18)

The king did not notice that three men did not bow to the statue. If it weren't for the Babylonian wise men who informed on Shadrach, Meshach, and Abed-Nego, they probably would have gotten away with it.

One gets the feeling the Babylonian wise men were only too happy to tell the king about the three friends' noncompliance. The fact that in their complaint they describe them as "some Jews whom you have set over the affairs of the province of Babylon" (Dan 3:12) indicates that they were motivated out of jealousy for the high position that these men occupy.

The charge—"they neither serve your gods nor worship the image of gold you have set up"—does not answer our question whether the statue represents the gods or the king since the image is named separately here, though it could be a specific example of not worshiping the gods.[1]

Nebuchadnezzar responds with intense anger and calls Shadrach, Meshach, and Abed-Nego to him. He tests them by bringing in the orchestra and has them play again. He warns them that if they do not bow then they will be thrown "immediately into a blazing furnace" (Dan 5:15).

Much consternation has been expressed over the years as to the availability of this blazing furnace out near the plains of Dura. We don't really know the location of his plain, but its name means "fortress." Thus, it may be a plain in the country outside the urban center. Who knows whether there was a metal-refining station nearby or something similar. The story does not depend on our answering the question of what exactly it was or how it operated. The way the men will be thrown in and observed, though, also raises questions. Not surprisingly, some recent scholars believe that the story is fictional, and rather than a real furnace, it was created for the story for dramatic effect. One scholar argues that it suggested itself to the imagination of the author from the phrase, "The iron-smelting furnace, out of Egypt" (Deut 4:20).[2] Beaulieu, however, cites an eighteenth-century BC letter that mentions the execution of people by putting them in a cook's oven as related to this story.[3] We will continue to read on though there is some opaqueness to the story probably caused by our historical distance.

Back to the story, the three faithful men don't even wait for the music to start to give Nebuchadnezzar his response. While there is some question about the specifics, there is no doubt about their refusal to bow. The doubt is over whether the men are certain that God is able and will definitely deliver them from the blazing furnace. The question centers on whether the Aramaic of Daniel 3:17 should be translated, "If we are thrown into the blazing furnace, the God we serve is able to deliver us from it, and he will deliver us from Your Majesty's hand," as the NIV translates it, or whether it should be translated, "If the God we serve is able to deliver us, then he will deliver us from the blazing furnace and from Your Majesty's hand," as the NIV footnote reads and similarly the NRSV.

There are unresolved issues in both of these proposed translations, but what is clear is that the three friends will not betray their God. Indeed, the second rendering may be an even more profound statement of their faith, since they will refuse the request even if they die in the fire.

We should pause here to acknowledge the importance of this point even before we move on to the deliverance. We have seen that the book of Daniel is trying to assure people who are living under persecution that they can not only survive but even thrive in spite of their suffering. That said, the book of Daniel is not a proof text for the prosperity gospel. Faithful people must be willing to die for their faith; indeed, as the history of God's people has shown time and time again, many faithful people have died as the result of persecution.

But not this time.

IN THE FIERY FURNACE (DAN 3:19-27)

The three men's response only served to intensify the king's anger. He grew hot himself and ordered the heating up of the furnace "seven times hotter than usual" (Dan 3:19). Indeed, the furnace was so hot that the soldiers who threw the fully clothed and bound men in were themselves incinerated.

Then something amazing happened. Nebuchadnezzar was the first one to see it. They threw in three men, but the king saw four in the furnace. The three men were not burning up in the fire, but four men were walking around. And the fourth "looks like a son of the gods" (Dan 3:25).

Nebuchadnezzar then called to Shadrach, Meshach, and Abed-Nego to come out, and then not only were they not burned but "the fire had not harmed their bodies, nor was a hair of their heads singed; their robes were not scorched, and there was no smell of fire on them" (Dan 3:27).

THE KING'S RESPONSE (DAN 3:28-30)

The king himself understood that this rescue from the fire could only come about through the intervention of the three men's God. When he called them out of the fire, he addressed them as "servants of the Most High God" (Dan 3:26), and now he praises that God.

He had earlier mocked them by saying, "What god will be able to rescue you from my hand?" (Dan 3:15), and now he knew. The God of Shadrach, Meshach, and Abed-Nego could so save them. It was their God who had sent "his angel" (Dan 3:28) into the fire to preserve their lives. And so this pagan king proclaims, "No other god can save in this way" (Dan 3:29).

Thus, anyone who threatens these three men will "be cut into pieces and their houses turned into piles of rubble" (Dan 3:29). Further, the king promoted the three friends to even higher positions within the empire (Dan 3:30).

CONCLUSION

In this first of two tales of court conflict, we see again that in spite of present difficulties (the three friends are accused and thrown into the fire), God is in control (he sends his angel to protect them), and he will have the final victory (the three friends emerge from the fire unscathed). While God's people must be willing to die for their faith under persecution, and sometimes they will, they can often not only survive but also thrive under the most difficult circumstances.

DISCUSSION QUESTIONS

1. What words would you use to describe Nebuchadnezzar in this chapter? What reaction do you have to Nebuchadnezzar both in the first part and the second part of the chapter?

2. What words would you use to describe the three friends in this chapter? What reaction do you have to them throughout the chapter?

3. What is the purpose of the frequent repetition of the long lists of officials and musical instruments in the chapter?

4. How do our two themes (in spite of present circumstances, God is in control and will have the final victory, and you can not only survive but thrive during oppression) present themselves to the reader in this chapter?

NINE

Daniel in the Lions' Den

Daniel 6

Our second tale of court conflict involves Daniel alone, and the story, as we said in the previous chapter, has similarities of plot with the story of the three friends and the fiery furnace. Daniel, like the three friends in that chapter, becomes the target of accusations brought by his Babylonian colleagues. He is sentenced to death, but God again sends an angel who delivers him from death. These similarities of plot, however, should not overshadow the differences, which we will observe in our interpretation of the chapter.

THE PLOT AGAINST DANIEL (DAN 6:1-9)

Darius, who had taken over the kingdom of Babylon (Dan 5:30), was now king.[1] In setting up his administrative bureaucracy, Darius appointed 120 satraps (provincial leaders) with three people over them, including Daniel, and Daniel so distinguished himself that Darius planned to appoint Daniel over them all. Thus, we see a difference between Daniel 3 and 6 in the benevolent attitude of the monarch, in this case Darius, toward Daniel, which contrasts with the anger that Nebuchadnezzar had toward the three friends.

Daniel's rise to power brought on the jealousy of the other leaders, who then plotted to undermine him. But at first they were stymied because they could find no dirt on him. He was clearly a person of integrity, as even his enemies were forced to admit.

Thus, his foes tried another angle. They knew that Daniel followed the law of his God and would not compromise that law even if it meant breaking the law of Darius. Thus, these schemers knew that the way to get Daniel in trouble was to create a situation where he would have to choose between the law of his God and the law of his king.

Accordingly, they suggested to the king that he promulgate a decree that all prayers for the next thirty days must be directed to Darius himself, not to any god or any other human beings. The penalty of noncompliance was to be thrown into a den of lions. Darius accepted the proposal.

On the surface, this decree is quite odd. The Persian/Median kings, as far as we know, did not consider themselves gods. And then, it is also strange that there is a thirty-day time limit on this statute. Why not a permanent change?

The best understanding, it seems to me, is that this statute appealed to Darius as a kind of loyalty test. He did not consider himself a god, but he is probably putting himself forward as a human mediator to the gods. Thus, one could communicate with the gods only by praying through him as an intercessor. If one did not do that, they exposed their disloyalty to the king. Notice then how this idea is similar to what was going on with Nebuchadnezzar's golden statue. These kings were likely somewhat insecure and were looking to out potential traitors who did not have the king as their ultimate leader.

The evil plot worked. It appealed to the king's pride and insecurity. He apparently did not have a clue that he was being set up.

THE TRAP SPRINGS (DAN 6:10-15)

The plot switches scenes from the royal court to Daniel's home. Notice how the narrator matter-of-factly describes Daniel's reaction. "Now when Daniel learned that the decree had been published, he went home to his upstairs room where the windows opened toward Jerusalem. Three times a day he got down on his knees and prayed, giving thanks to his God, just as he had done before" (Dan 6:10). We don't hear about his thinking process or his emotional reaction, just his continued obedience to pray, not to or through Darius but rather directly to his God.

He continues praying in this manner, but note he neither makes a public protest by praying in the street nor is he so private that he only prays behind locked doors. He just follows his usual pattern of praying three times a day toward Jerusalem (and the location of the now-destroyed temple). His window is open! He could easily be discovered.

And, of course, he was caught. He was, according to the narrator, calling on God for help presumably because he knows what was going to happen. The Babylonian administrators went directly to the king to inform on Daniel. They shrewdly began by reminding the king of his decree before naming Daniel as the culprit. They get him to reiterate the decree, and the king himself states, "The decree stands—in accordance with the law of the Medes and Persians, which cannot be repealed" (Dan 6:12). Then they tell the king the name of the culprit—Daniel, his favorite. At this point, the king realizes his mistake. Here we learn of his emotional reaction: "When the king heard this, he was greatly distressed; he was determined to rescue Daniel and made every effort until sundown to save him" (Dan 6:14).

But the conspirators have him blocked in—or so they think. They reminded him of what he had just said: "Remember, Your Majesty, that according to the law of the Medes and Persians no decree or edict that the king issues can be changed" (Dan 6:15).

DANIEL THROWN INTO THE LIONS' DEN (DAN 6:16-24)

How often does a king who orders an execution express the hope that the condemned will survive? Not often, but Darius's concern for Daniel expresses itself with such a wish that Daniel's God would protect him as they threw him into the pit with lions.

Escape for Daniel was cut off by a stone placed over the mouth of the pit and sealed with the signet rings of the king and his nobles so no one could open the pit without being detected. The king, clearly distraught, returned to his palace and spent an anxious night without food, entertainment, or sleep.

The next morning the king hurried to the lion pit to see whether or not Daniel survived. The king himself testifies to the reality that only a powerful God could have preserved Daniel's life that evening: "Daniel, servant of the living God, has your God, whom you serve continually, been able to rescue you from the lions?" (Dan 6:20).

In his response, Daniel too praised his God. He recounted that, as with the three friends in the fiery furnace, God had sent his angel to close the mouths of the lions so that he could emerge unscathed.

Notice how he takes this as proof of his innocence. We know that he actually did not obey the king's decree, but he understands that this was not a rebellion against the king himself. Daniel knows that he would obey the king unless it conflicts with what he knows God wants of him. Daniel would have seen this as a question of obedience to the king or to God, and in such a situation, Daniel chooses obedience to God.

We can understand the chapter better if we become aware of the ancient Near Eastern practice of the ordeal. In certain situations, a person's guilt or innocence is established by undergoing some type of ordeal. In Mesopotamia, the most widely practiced was the river ordeal. Here a suspected person was thrown into the river, and if they died, then they were guilty (and in this way executed), but if they were innocent, they would survive.[2]

The Bible does not mention water ordeals like this connected with the law, but many scholars see the water ordeal as behind the accounts of Noah's flood and the crossing of the sea, where the guilty are punished by the waters but the innocent survive. But there is one ordeal in the law, a drink ordeal (Num 5:11-31), where a woman suspected of adultery drinks from a cup prepared by the priest. If she is guilty, her womb miscarries.[3] So ordeals were known broadly in the ancient Near East, and Daniel's survival demonstrates his innocence.

But what of the guilty—namely, those conspirators who set Daniel and Darius up in the first place? They were thrown into the pit along with their families, and they were killed before their bodies even hit the floor.[4] Apparently the lions did not refrain from eating Daniel out of lack of hunger.

DARIUS PRAISES DANIEL'S GOD AND
DANIEL PROSPERS (DAN 6:25-28)

In this last of the six stories that constitute the first part of the book of Daniel, we end with Darius's praise of God and also a narrative note that Daniel prospered during the early Persian period. Like Nebuchadnezzar before him (Dan 2:47; 3:28-29; 4:1-3, 34-35), Darius, a pagan Persian king, praises Daniel's God. He acknowledges that he is a living God whose kingdom will never end. He is capable of miraculous rescues attested by his rescue of Daniel from the lions (Dan 6:26-27).

While it is unlikely that either Nebuchadnezzar or Darius ever became a true worshiper of Yahweh alone, the fact that they acknowledge the God of Daniel as powerful would speak volumes to oppressed Jews through history. After all, in spite of present difficulties (Daniel accused and thrown into the lions' den), God is in control (he sent his angel to shut the mouths of the lions), and he will have the final victory (Daniel emerges untouched). His oppressors, on the other hand, find a terrible end. And Daniel, as he prospers, becomes again a sign that God's oppressed people not only can survive but can thrive in a hostile culture while remaining totally faithful to their God.

CONCLUSION

We now have reviewed all six narratives, though not in canonical order. Daniel 6, like the other five chapters, while different, all carry the same basic message. In spite of present circumstances (in this case being set up by jealous colleagues and sentenced to death), God is in control (he keeps the lions from killing Daniel), and he will have the final victory (Daniel emerges unscathed from the lions' den, while his detractors are killed). Again, this message would be a tremendous encouragement to later readers who themselves were living under the oppression of those who hated them.

DISCUSSION QUESTIONS

1. Describe the similarities and differences between the story of the three friends in the fiery furnace (Dan 3) and Daniel in the lions' den (Dan 6).

2. Describe in your own words how the main theme (in spite of present difficulties, God is in control and will have the final victory) works itself out in Daniel 6.

3. Describe in your own words how the secondary theme (you can not only survive but thrive under oppression) works itself out in Daniel 6.

4. Describe the personality of King Darius in this chapter and how he reacts to the various events narrated. How does he compare to Nebuchadnezzar and Belshazzar in the previous chapters?

TEN

"One like a Son of Man"

Daniel 7

The first of the four visions of the second part of the book introduces us to the vivid and striking imagery characteristic of apocalyptic literature. To a modern readership, this figurative language seems quite fantastic and even strange. When read it in its ancient context, however, many of the images have ancient roots that would have made the message more immediately clear to its original readers. Unfortunately, modern readers who do not understand this ancient context are often misled by some popular contemporary readers who are able to exploit our modern distance from the language of these chapters (see more in chap. 2).

Each of the four visions in the second half of the book is self-contained. They present their own account of future events. But that does not mean that they don't overlap, treating at least in part the same time period. They all start in Daniel's present and stretch our vision into the future. Some, but not all, take us to the end of history. Along the way, they treat different parts of the story with different levels of detail.

Daniel 7 is the first of these divinely given visions. As we will see, this vision is an example of one that takes us to the end of history, though we will mention those who dispute this idea. Daniel 7, with its striking figurative depiction of evil kingdoms and divine intervention, may be the best known of the four visions. It is, after all, the one that is most often alluded to in the New Testament (see chap. 16).

THE VISION (DAN 7:1-14)

Beast-like human figures (Dan 7:1-8). The narrator sets Daniel's dream in the "first year of Belshazzar" (Dan 7:1). In our earlier historical review (see chap. 2), we noted that Belshazzar became his father Nabonidus's coregent after the latter moved his palace out of Babylon to Tayma. We do not know exactly when this occurred, but we surmise that it was a few years after Nabonidus became king (556 BC) and a few years before the writing on the wall episode (Dan 6) and the end of the Babylonian Empire (539 BC).

The message of this vision was not meant for the Babylonians though. Rather, God through the vision is speaking directly to Daniel and through Daniel to God's faithful people. Though the vision is terrifying, the ultimate message to this audience is one of tremendous hope.

The first part of the vision describes four horrifying beasts arising out of a chaotic sea. While the vision mystifies a modern twenty-first-century audience from the start, much of the figurative language would have immediately resonated with the original audience, though they too would have needed the angelic interpretation that follows the description of the vision to plumb more deeply into its meaning (Dan 7:15-27).

Daniel begins by describing the setting of the vision, which is at a shore looking out at the sea whose waves are being whipped up by the four winds of heaven. The four winds would be winds coming from all four directions, thus producing a scene of chaos.

By the time Daniel had his vision, the sea was a long-established symbol of chaos and even the forces of evil in the broader ancient Near East. The Babylonian (Enuma Elish) and the Canaanite (Baal Myth) accounts of creation all pictured the creator god as creating order out of chaos by controlling the waters.[1] The Bible, too, often describes creation in this way (Job 38:8-11; Ps 24:1-2; Prov 8:22-30; perhaps even

Gen 1:1-2).[2] In addition, the psalmists (e.g., Ps 29:10) and the prophets (e.g., Nah 1:4) often depicted chaos through the figure of the sea.

Thus, not only the waters but its monsters were associated with evil. One only has to think of Leviathan (Job 41; Ps 74:12-17; Is 27:1) as an example. Here in Daniel's vision, we have four beast-like monsters emerging from the sea. A Jewish reader would have an immediate gut-wrenching reaction to such a vision. But worse, these are not any ordinary sea monsters. Their individual descriptions are horrifying.

The first one is a hybrid beast. It was like a lion, but it had wings like an eagle. Ultimately it stands on its feet like a human being (Dan 7:4). We begin with the observation that hybrids of any sort were repulsive to the original readers. Remember that the Torah forbade mixtures of all sorts, whether material or of seeds in a field (Lev 19:19). Further, the best explanation for why certain animals were considered clean and others not clean (and therefore inappropriate to eat) was because the former were normal to their environments (like a fish with fins and scales) and not abnormal for its environment (like a lobster that looks like a land creature living in the sea). Thus, the very hybrid nature of the first creature would have been nightmarish to the original audience. The fact that this animal-like creature took on a human form would have been particularly upsetting.

The second beast was not a hybrid, but it frightens in a different way (Dan 7:5). The creature is like a bear, one of the most dangerous animals known to humans. And this one is pictured in a violent pose. Lying on one of its sides, it was gnawing on three ribs. An unidentified voice then orders it, "Get up [from its prone position] and eat your fill of flesh!" (Dan 7:5).

Daniel's attention then is directed to a third beast, another hybrid (Dan 7:6), again a beast of prey ("like a leopard") combined with a bird's wings. This bird-leopard was abnormal in another way: it had four heads! This beast is said to have been "given authority to rule."

Finally, Daniel sees the fourth beast rising out of the sea (Dan 7:7-8). The first three were indeed horrible, but this beast took it to a new level. It was "different from all the former beasts" (Dan 7:7). The focus of the vision is on this fourth beast; the first three were just the beginning.

This beast is primarily different in the fact that it is not compared to any known animal in human experience. It is not like a lion or an eagle or a bear or a leopard or a bird or even a human. The only physical description we get in the vision itself is that it has "iron teeth," while later in the interpretation we will hear that it has "iron teeth and bronze claws" (Dan 7:19). Daniel describes his understanding of what this metallic beast's description communicates by saying that it was "terrifying and frightening and very powerful" (Dan 7:7).

The last important detail of the description of this fourth beast is the fact that it has horns. Animal horns were a well-known biblical symbol of strength. While most animals have two horns at most, this beast had ten. The number ten itself is often, and certainly here, used symbolically rather than straightforwardly. It connotes a large number. But then Daniel sees another horn break through. This horn is little, but it still manages to displace three of the original horns. Amazingly, this little horn has human-like characteristics, having eyes and the ability to utter proud words.

Thus ends the first part of the vision. But before we hear the interpretation of its meaning, we turn next to the second part of the vision itself.

Human-like divine figures (7:9-14). In Daniel 7:9-14 the setting of the vision abruptly changes. No longer are we at the seashore where we observe the emergence of horrifying and destructive beasts. We are now in a courtroom and are first introduced to a figure referred to as the Ancient of Days.

The scene is a courtroom, but this is not any ordinary courtroom. The centerpiece is the throne of the Ancient of Days, a title that indicates a person of great antiquity. As such he is described as having white hair. He is also wearing a white robe. His throne is engulfed in flames, fire often associated with the appearance of God, and indeed, this figure can only be taken to refer to God himself. A river of fire flows from this throne. Fire not only warms and illuminates but also burns. Here God is pictured as a judge ready to render judgment ("The court was seated, and the books were opened," Dan 7:10). God's angelic servants surround him by the thousands.

The object of the judgment of the Ancient of Days is implicit but made clear in verses 11-12. The boastful words of the destructive little horn had drawn the attention of the Ancient of Days with the result that the fourth beast, which hosted the horn, was destroyed. Interestingly, and somewhat enigmatically, we learn that the first three beasts were still alive and allowed to survive for a period of time.

But then something totally unexpected occurs. Into the presence of the Ancient of Days steps "one like a son of man, coming with the clouds of heaven" (7:13). Who is this figure? While the language and imagery of this verse would have been familiar to the ancient reader (though strange to us), the implications would have shocked them.

First, we should realize that "son of man" is a phrase that occurs a number of times in the Old Testament, particularly in the book of Ezekiel (2:1, 3, 6, and throughout the book), and always means "human being." But notice this is one "*like* a human being," not a human being per se. And his association, though not identification, with humanity is clear from the fact that this human-like figure is accompanied by the clouds of heaven. In other words, this person is a cloud rider, a sure indication of divinity.

In the first place, in the broader ancient Near East, cloud riding was the function of storm gods like Baal, who was often called "cloud rider" in the Ugaritic myths that describe his exploits.[3] By the time of Daniel, many Old Testament texts had appropriated this description and applied it to God (Ps 18:1-9; 68:4; 103:3; Is 19:1; Nah 1:3). Thus, to ancient readers this human-like figure was God himself riding into the presence of the Ancient of Days, also God himself, after achieving victory over the beasts. No wonder this passage is cited so often in the New Testament in reference to Jesus, God's Son and God himself (more on this in chapter 16).

But for now, restricting ourselves to an Old Testament reader's perspective, we should notice that the vision ends with the Ancient of

Days conferring great honor on the one like the son of man. Indeed, "he was given (presumably by the Ancient of Days) authority, glory and sovereign power; all nations and peoples of every language worshipped him. His dominion is an everlasting dominion that will not pass away, and his kingdom is one that will never be destroyed" (7:14).

THE ANGELIC INTERPRETATION OF
THE DREAM (DAN 7:15-28)

Daniel has been perplexed and disturbed by this vision. He thus, still seemingly in the vision, turns to "one of those standing there" (Dan 7:16), perhaps one of the thousands of heavenly beings surrounding the Ancient of Days, to get the meaning of what he has seen.

The angel begins with an overall interpretation. He starts by simply saying that the four beasts are four kings who will appear in earthly history, but then "the holy people of the Most High . . . will possess it forever—yes, for ever and ever" (v. 18). In other words, while beastly human kingdoms will oppress the people of God (in spite of present difficulties), God is in control, and he will have the final victory.

But Daniel wants more details, particularly about the fourth beast and the little horn. The angel obliges him, but only to a point.

In verses 19-22, Daniel recounts what he saw and what he understood about the fourth beast. He knows that this beast was particularly frightening and devastating, different from all the rest in that it is never compared to any known animal but simply described in metallic terms. He also wanted to know about the meaning of the horns and in particular the little horn that had human-like features (eyes and a mouth) that uprooted three of the ten horns.

At this point we learn a detail about the violence of the little horn that we did not learn in the description of the vision itself. For example, we learn that the object of the little horn's violence was "the holy people" (v. 21). These people, of course, are none other than those, like Daniel, who were among the faithful, and, shockingly, the little horn was winning! That is until the Ancient of Days rendered judgment, and then they, "the holy people," would possess the kingdom.

The angel responds by filling in more details but, interestingly, still keeping matters somewhat opaque. He says that the fourth beast is a fourth kingdom and that the ten horns are ten kings of that kingdom. The little horn is a king that will arise and will direct his ill-will against the holy people. He will interrupt the "set times" (perhaps ritual times like Sabbaths and festivals) as well as the holy people's laws. This will take place for a period, described as a "time, times [or two times] and half a time" (v. 25), which appears to be an intentionally enigmatic statement (see comments on the use and purpose of statements about time in chap. 3).[4]

But, according to the interpreting angel, this is not the end of the story. Turning to the second half of the vision, he notes the judgment that will be rendered on the oppressive king represented by the little horn. His power will be removed and given to the "holy people" whom he had oppressed. But then finally, "his [presumably the one like the son of man] kingdom will be an everlasting kingdom, and all rulers will worship and obey him" (7:27). Daniel reacts to this interpretation with increased concern, but he keeps it to himself.

CONCLUSION

The message of the vision is quite clear, particularly in the light of its angelic interpretation. God's people are living under the oppression of violent human kingdoms, represented by the beasts, and their kings (the horns of the fourth beast). As the vision extends into the future beyond the time of Daniel, it envisions a particularly evil and violent ruler (the little horn) who will bring special suffering on God's people. While having success (for a time, times), that success will first be curbed (and half a time) and finally brought to an end by the intrusion of God the warrior (the one like the son of man riding on the clouds of heaven) at the direction of God the judge (the Ancient of Days).

Daniel and his contemporary audience are living in the midst of the oppression of the beasts. The temptation is to despair. This vision as well as those that follow pull back the curtains and reveal that the beasts will not have the final victory.

DISCUSSION QUESTIONS

1. Describe the nature of apocalyptic literature as exemplified by Daniel 7. What appeals to you about this form of literature? What doesn't appeal?

2. Apocalyptic literature often seems mysterious and difficult to interpret. Why do you think the author wrote in such a form?

3. What do the beasts represent in the vision?

4. How does the main theme of the book (in spite of present circumstances, God is in control and will have the final victory) work itself out in this chapter?

5. The two central figures in the second half of the vision are "the Ancient of Days" and "the one like a son of man." What is their role in the vision, and what do they represent? What is particularly striking about their relationship?

ELEVEN

A Ram and a Goat

Daniel 8

Two years after the vision recorded in Daniel 7, Daniel received a second vision. Daniel himself tells the reader about the vision in the first person throughout and recounts the interpretation supplied by a heavenly being. He briefly dates this experience to the third year of Belshazzar (Dan 8:1). Since we don't know when Belshazzar began his coregency with Nabonidus, we can only approximately date the vision to sometime between 550 and 539 BC, toward the end of the Babylonian Empire.

As we will see, this vision, like the previous one, is highly symbolic and needs interpretation. The connection to history is made more concretely to specific nations, so there is not the same disagreement among scholars that we saw in the previous chapter as to which nations the figures point to. Still, as will become clear, the overall theme remains the same: in spite of present difficulties, God is in control, and he will have the final victory.

THE VISION BY THE ULAI CANAL (DAN 8:2-14)

In this vision, Daniel finds himself by the Ulai Canal near Susa. Susa is one of the main cities of Persia, which, as we will see, plays a central role in the vision. The setting outside the city allows space for the action that will follow in the vision.

At first, a lone ram appears (Dan 8:3-4). Like any ram it has two horns, but this ram is distinctive in that one of its horns is longer than the other. The significance of this and other details of the vision will become obvious in the interpretation that follows. Then this ram strikes out in every direction, and nothing can stop it. No other animal could challenge it, and so the ram "became great" (Dan 8:4).

That is until the appearance of a goat "with a prominent horn between its eyes" (Dan 8:5-8). This goat attacked the ram from the west and broke off the ram's two horns. Without its horns the ram was defenseless and soon destroyed. Now the goat "became very great" (Dan 8:8). But then during its height, the goat's horn was broken off and replaced by four other horns.

Now the vision focuses on the horns, and the attention turns to yet another horn that grew out of one of the four new ones (Dan 8:9-14). This horn grew south and east toward the "Beautiful Land"; the fact that the devastation that follows concerns the sanctuary of the Lord and its rituals makes it clear at this point that we are talking about Judah.

Indeed, the power of this horn is such that it even challenges the powers of heaven since it touched the host of heaven and even threw down and trampled some of the "starry host," which references the angelic realm. It affected the worship of God by suspending the daily sacrifice and throwing down the sanctuary (temple). God's people become another victim of this powerful horn. Interestingly this devastation is said to be caused by "rebellion," presumably by the people of God themselves.

At the end of the vision, Daniel reports that he heard a conversation between two angels or "holy ones." One asks the other "how long" will this last? How long will "the daily sacrifice, the rebellion that causes desolation, the surrender of the sanctuary and the trampling underfoot of the LORD's people" last (Dan 8:13)? The response: "It will take 2,300 evenings and mornings; then the sanctuary will be reconsecrated" (Dan 8:14).

THE INTERPRETATION (DAN 8:15-27)

From Daniel's sixth-century-BC perspective, none of this would have been clear to him. He needed heavenly help to understand. We will see that this vision describes events that occur between the time of Daniel and the mid-second century BC. Thus, I will be able to fill in some details not provided by the angelic interpreter but will be careful to point out when we go beyond the information that the angel provides.

While Daniel is trying to understand the vision, he notices someone who looks like a man standing near him, who turns out to be the angel Gabriel, whom we know from elsewhere in Daniel (Dan 9:21) as well as the New Testament (Lk 1:19, 26) as the angel commissioned to speak on behalf of God. An unidentified voice, probably to be understood as God's, orders him to inform Daniel of the meaning of the vision. Gabriel thus begins by telling him that the vision concerns the "time of the end" (Dan 8:17), though it is not immediately clear whether he means the end of time or the end of the present oppression or perhaps some other end.

Moving to the content of the vision, he gets right to the point where he identifies the first animal, the ram with the two horns, as the combined nations of Media and Persia. The goat is Greece and the prominent horn is its first king, who later readers would know refers to Alexander the Great (356–323 BC), though that identification would be beyond the knowledge of someone who lived in the sixth century BC. The breaking off of the first horn represented Alexander's death at a young age, and the four horns that replaced it the four generals—often referred to as the Diadochi—who divided the vast Greek Empire between themselves when Alexander died.

The violent and destructive horn at the end of the vision that would wreak havoc on the people of God and their worship is here described as emerging from the four horns and as a "fierce-looking king, a master of intrigue." This king will rise up "when rebels have become completely wicked" (Dan 8:23). He will oppress the "holy people" (Dan 8:24), those who are God's faithful followers, and will even challenge God himself, "the Prince of princes" (Dan 8:25). But in spite of his success, "he will be destroyed, but not by human power" (Dan 8:25).

Gabriel then announces that the vision of the "evenings and mornings" (Dan 8:26) is true, by which he points back to the "2,300 evenings and mornings" (Dan 8:14) that will take place between the desecration and the reconsecration of the sanctuary—that is, the temple.

Daniel's reaction is interesting. His energy is obviously spent by the experience, and he still does not understand. After all, the events so described are in the far future. That said, he was not completely debilitated and "went about the king's business" (Dan 8:27).

CONCLUSION

We can understand Daniel's confusion. God gave him the vision before the end of the Babylonian Empire. Persia and Greece were both on the rise at that time, but they were certainly not the powers that they would become in the following decades and centuries. The four horns and the little horn would have been completely unknown to a sixth-century Daniel, but we know the little horn that became large is Antiochus Epiphanes, who in the mid-second century BC brought unprecedented persecution on the faithful people of God while some of their countrymen (the rebels in the vision) became his collaborators. We will have more to say about Antiochus at a later point, but he culminates the anticipated persecution of God's faithful (in spite of present difficulty).

That said, the vision sees a determinate end to the persecution. He will be able to despoil the temple but only for a limited period—2,300 evenings and mornings. There is some ambiguity in this number,[1] but I suggest it is intentional so that this number, while communicating a decisive end, cannot be used to determine a date on a calendar. What is certain is that it is coming to an end. Because, after all, God is in control, and he will have the final victory.

DISCUSSION QUESTIONS

1. How does this vision fit into the overall purpose and theme of the book of Daniel (in spite of present circumstances, God is in control and will have the final victory)?

2. What and/or who do the beasts represent in this vision?

3. How does this vision relate to the vision in Daniel 7?

TWELVE

Seventy Weeks

The Exile Continues: Daniel 9

D aniel 9 is a vision of a different sort than the first two found in Daniel 7 and 8. Those were visions with fantastic imagery that seem to have come while Daniel was asleep or in a trance-like state. This "vision" (as it is only called in Dan 9:23) arises from Daniel's reading of Scripture, in particular the book of Jeremiah.

This event takes place during the first year of the reign of Darius over Babylon, whose identity we have pondered earlier and found mysterious (see chap. 2) but about whose time period we have little doubt. The result is that whomever Darius is (Cyrus himself? Someone Cyrus put in charge of Babylon?), we know that his first year ruling would have been 539 BC.

We turn now to explore the circumstances of this unusual vision as well as its meaning.

DANIEL READING JEREMIAH (DAN 9:1-3)

Daniel again speaks in the first person and begins by reporting that he was reading Scripture, specifically the book of Jeremiah. While there are many times in which later Old Testament Scripture alludes to earlier Scripture, this occasion is a rare instance where a later author names a specific earlier one.

If the date for this event is 539 BC as we suggested, Jeremiah is only removed from Daniel by a couple of generations. The earlier prophet begins receiving his prophecy in Josiah's thirteenth year (626 BC), and God continues to speak to him until the fall of Jerusalem (586 BC; Jer 1:1-3) and even beyond the exile for a few years (Jer 40–45).[1]

While we neither know how Daniel got ahold of a copy of Jeremiah or even whether it was a final version of the book as we have it today, we are struck by how he understands that it is Scripture, part of the authoritative writings considered the Word of God. And we know that he is reading from a section of Jeremiah that we know as 25:1-14, which comes from the fourth year of Jehoiakim, the first year of Nebuchadnezzar's reign (605 BC). This is also the approximate date of the time when Daniel and the three friends were taken into captivity (Dan 1:1-2).

Daniel's attention is riveted on God's message to Jeremiah that, because of the sin of God's people, "This whole country will become a desolate wasteland, and these nations will serve the king of Babylon seventy years. But when the seventy years are fulfilled, I will punish the king of Babylon and his nation, the land of the Babylonians . . . and will make it desolate forever" (Jer 25:11-12; also 29:10).

Daniel is reading about the seventy-year exile and realizes that that time period may be drawing to a close in the near future. After all, he was taken to Babylon around 605 BC, and Daniel 9 is set in Darius's first year, around 539 BC. Of course, the number seventy may not be an exact year since it is a multiple of seven—the number of completion—and ten, but still he may be thinking that the time of the exile is drawing to a close. This expectation may still be the case even if he is thinking that the seventy years started with the year that Nebuchadnezzar took Jerusalem and destroyed the temple (586 BC).

DANIEL'S PRAYER FOR RESTORATION (DAN 9:4-19)

Whatever exactly is going through Daniel's mind, he turns immediately to God in prayer. He knows that restoration will not be automatic and the exile was caused by the sins of God's people, so he, with fasting and other signs of contrition (wearing sackcloth and ashes), turns to God with prayers of petition.

It is likely Daniel knew Solomon's prayer at the time of the dedication of the temple when he foresaw an occasion like this one:

> When they [the people of God] sin against you—for there is no one who does not sin—and you become angry with them and give them over to their enemies, who take them captive to their own lands, far away or near; and if they have a change of heart in the land where they are held captive, and repent and plead with you in the land of their captors and say, "We have sinned, we have done wrong, we have acted wickedly"; and if they turn back to you with all their heart and soul in the land of their enemies who took them captive, and pray to you toward the land you gave their ancestors, toward the city you have chosen and the temple I have built for your Name; then from heaven, your dwelling place, hear their prayer and their plea, and uphold their cause. And forgive your people, who have sinned against you; forgive all the offenses they have committed against you, and cause their captors to show them mercy; for they are your people and your inheritance, whom you brought out of Egypt, out of that iron-smelting furnace. (1 Kings 8:46-51; see also Lev 26:40-45; Deut 30:1-10)

Mark Boda, one of today's leading experts on this type of communal penitentiary prayer in the Old Testament, analyzes the component parts of Daniel's prayer as follows: "The prayer creatively interweaves several components key to this prayer tradition: confession of Israel's sin, praise of God's character and action, articulation of Israel's predicament, and request for God's intervention." We follow his outline of Daniel's prayer in what follows.[2]

Confession of Israel's sin (Dan 9:5-6, 7c, 8b, 9b-11a, 11c, 13b, 14c, 15b, 16c). Throughout his prayer, Daniel acknowledges that God's people are in their present sad condition because of their sin. They have broken the Torah, and they have not listened to the prophets.

As a result, the curses of the covenant (Lev 26; Deut 27–28) have come upon them.

Notice that Daniel speaks in the first person plural. He does not distance himself from Israel's sin but includes himself in the community. He prays on behalf of his people and for sins past and present.

Praise of God's character and action (Dan 9:4, 7a, 9a, 14b, 15a, 16a, 18b). While in his prayer Daniel emphasizes Judah's sin, he also speaks of God's righteousness and mercy and the acts that have flowed from them in the past, particularly the rescue from Egypt at the time of the exodus. Israel's punishment is a righteous act of God. They deserved it, Daniel admits, but now he asks God to act on his mercy and rescue them as he did the Israelites out of Egypt.

Articulation of Israel's predicament (Dan 9:7b, 8a, 12-13a, 14a, 16d). Because of their sin, the curses of the covenant have come on Israel, and they are scattered throughout the nations. Daniel himself, of course, is an early example of this because he has been in the city of Babylon for almost seventy years. As a result of this scattering, God's people as well as their city, Jerusalem, are "an object of scorn" (Dan 9:16).

Request for God's intervention (Dan 9:17-19). Daniel ends his prayer with an impassioned plea for mercy. He asks that God stop their punishment and restore them and the sanctuary in Jerusalem. He does not ask God to rescue them because of their own merit but because "your city and your people bear your Name" (Dan 9:19).

THE RESPONSE: THE SEVENTY "SEVENS" (DAN 9:20-27)

Daniel gets an immediate answer to his prayer, though it was not exactly what he was hoping for. The answer came in the form of Gabriel, God's angelic messenger, whom we have already met (Dan 8:16). He answers his prayer by providing an interpretation of Jeremiah's word about a seventy-year exile.

Gabriel begins by saying, "Seventy 'sevens' are decreed for your people" (Dan 9:24). Thus right from the start it appears that the exile will not definitely stop after seventy years, but it will be a longer period of time. This is the period of time necessary to "finish transgression, to

put an end to sin, to atone for wickedness, to bring in everlasting righteousness, to seal up vision and prophecy and to anoint the Most Holy
Place" (Dan 9:24).

Let's remember that the first year that Persia defeated Babylon was
likely the first year of Darius (539 BC). This year was also the one in
which Cyrus the Great of Persia issued his decree allowing the Jews to
return to Jerusalem (2 Chron 36:22-23; Ezra 1:1-4). Daniel was almost
assuredly aware of this, and in one important sense, the exile moved
to a different stage.

But Daniel must have been thinking of something more than the
return of some of the exiles from Babylon to Judah. The people of God
were still under the domination of a foreign power, not Babylon but
Persia. Judah was not at this time again an independent kingdom nor
was the temple yet rebuilt.

Thus, Daniel's hope was that the exile would come to a definitive
end, but Gabriel's message was that it was not yet time for that to
happen. On the negative side, transgression, sin, and wickedness was
not yet at an end or sufficiently atoned for. And on the other hand,
"everlasting righteousness" had not yet come to the people of God, nor
had the Most Holy Place been reconsecrated (anointed). Thus during
this time, vision and prophecy would be sealed up, not revealed.

Gabriel's final words to Daniel are enigmatic indeed, at least to us.
We don't know what Daniel himself understood of the words recorded
in Daniel 9:25-27 because he gives no recorded response. But to us,
they are difficult and thus have been the subject of multiple interpretations and overinterpretations.

To describe what Gabriel says without trying to interpret it, Daniel
takes the seventy "sevens" and divides them into periods of time. The
first period of time is from the moment there is a decree to rebuild
Jerusalem until the time of the "Anointed One." This period is said to
last for sixty-nine of the seventy "sevens," which itself is divided into
two parts, seven "sevens" and sixty-two "sevens."

Our difficulty with interpreting Gabriel's interpretation of the
seventy years of Jeremiah begins with the question of what are the

"sevens." Are they years? Perhaps so, since the interpretation is based on the seventy-year exile, but it is not absolutely certain that they are. And if they are years, does that mean they are actual years, or are they symbolic numbers (seven is certainly often used in a symbolic fashion) that cannot then be plugged into a timetable of the future? Accordingly, I believe that we should exercise great caution and avoid doing so.

The next issue is that there is debate whether we can actually determine today when the decree went out to rebuild Jerusalem. There are several possibilities. This rebuilding is described as involving "streets and a trench" (Dan 9:25), but when that happened we are unsure. Is this a reference to the Cyrus Decree that allowed Sheshbazzar and Zerubbabel to lead the initial return of deported Jews to Jerusalem to rebuild the temple (539 BC; see Ezra 1)? Or is it fulfilled later when the Persian king Artaxerxes allowed Nehemiah to return to Jerusalem and rebuild the wall (445 BC; see Neh 2)? Is it some other time?

And then there is the question of the identity of the "Anointed One." First, realize that the Hebrew does not capitalize the title, but modern translations sometimes do to imply that it might point to Jesus, but it is not at all clear that it does. Those who think it is Jesus believe that the period of the first sixty-nine sevens equals approximately 483 years (seven times sixty-nine years) and then try to find a date around 483 years before the death of Jesus to connect the rebuilding of Jerusalem.

But then what about the last period of "sevens"? During this time, there will be war and desolations. The "people of the ruler" (Dan 9:26) will destroy the city and the sanctuary, but who is the ruler? Whoever it is, he will confirm a covenant with the many (people, we assume). In the middle of his period of time (the final seven), he will stop sacrifice, presumably at the temple, and set up an abomination that causes desolation there. All this will happen, according to Gabriel, until the ruler's end comes.

WHAT ARE WE TO MAKE OF ALL THIS?
WHAT IS CLEAR AND WHAT IS NOT?

What is clear is that Gabriel is telling Daniel that the end of the exile is not coming any time soon. It will continue even if there are some improvements to their corporate life. But even with improvements, there will still be much turmoil and leaders who will cause trouble for the proper worship of God. But even so, there will be an end to this turmoil. The period of the seventy "sevens" will come to an end. The figure identified as the ruler who brings havoc on the temple and its sacrifices will come to an end.

CONCLUSION

We need to be honest when we interpret a text like Daniel 9. Not all passages are equally clear to us, and it is actually not all that obvious whether the text would have been more clear to Daniel or to those who were the original audience of this book. In other words, the passage, particularly that concerning the seventy "sevens," may well be intentionally ambiguous to communicate that the exile will continue but will have a future, definitive end without giving the type of information that would allow the reader to construct a chronology of the future.

In short, what is clear is that the exile will continue, and it will come to an eventual end. In this way, we again learn that in spite of present difficulties (God's people still live under foreign oppression), God is in control, and he will have the final victory.

What is not clear is the timing of the end. Like elsewhere, as we have and will see in Daniel, the seventy "sevens" are not given for us to set an apocalyptic timetable. We should resist the effort to do so and ignore those who do. What is sufficient to understand is that even though the exile will continue (in spite of present difficulties), God is in control, and he will have the final victory.

DISCUSSION QUESTIONS

1. Daniel repents for the sins that led to the conquest of Jerusalem and the exile though Daniel himself did not participate in that sin. What does that tell us about prayers of confession? Does Daniel's prayer teach us anything about our own prayers today?

2. While God's word to Jeremiah suggests the exile will last seventy years, Gabriel tells him it will continue to last for seventy "sevens." How do you reconcile these divine words to Jeremiah and Daniel?

3. Do you agree that the divine word to Daniel concerning the seventy "sevens" is intentionally ambiguous? Why or why not? If not, why do you think there are so many different interpretations of how it fits into a calendar of future events?

4. How does the central theme of the book (in spite of present difficulties, God is in control and will have the final victory) play out in this chapter?

THIRTEEN

"Yet He Will Come to His End"

Daniel 10:1–12:4

The fourth and final vision of Daniel takes place at the last mention of a date in the book of Daniel—namely, "in the third year of Cyrus king of Persia" (10:1). We assume that the date refers to Cyrus's rule over Babylon (not when he began ruling Persia per se), which he conquered in 539 BC. Accordingly, Daniel experienced this vision sometime around 536 BC.

Not only is this vision the last one but also it is the longest, particularly since it receives a lengthy narrative introduction. The whole of chapter 10 describes Daniel's meeting with heavenly beings who assist him in the interpretation of his disturbing vision. Here the reader is given one of the most penetrating depictions of actions in the heavenly realms among the angels that we have anywhere in the Old Testament. In Daniel 11:1–12:4 then we have a description and an interpretation of the vision itself. This vision, particularly its final part (Dan 12:1-4), takes the reader further into the future than any of the previous visions and provides what is commonly thought to be the fullest description of the afterlife in all the Old Testament.

DANIEL HAS A VISION AND MEETS
HIS INTERPRETER (DAN 10)

The narrator, who has not let his presence be known since Daniel 7:1, introduces the episode that is then recounted in the first person by Daniel beginning in Daniel 10:2. The narrator refers to Daniel by his Hebrew name though also takes note of the Babylonian name given to him by Nebuchadnezzar. He remarks that Daniel received a revelation (a message from God) and that the understanding of the revelation would come about through a vision. Moreover, we are informed that this message was "true" and told that the subject was a "great war" (Dan 10:1).

It is no wonder then that Daniel was deeply disturbed and not able to enjoy the ordinary pleasures of his daily life. For three weeks he was not able to eat or drink his normal diet of choice food, meat, or wine. He used no lotions that would hydrate his skin in the dry desert of Mesopotamia. We earlier remarked on this passage to demonstrate that Daniel's more restricted diet of vegetables and water was only during the period of his training and therefore could not be in reference to any kind of religious abstinence (see chap. 4 on Dan 1).

Daniel then recounted what took place on the "twenty-fourth day of the first month" (Dan 10:4) of presumably Cyrus's third year. He was on the shore of the Tigris River, the northeastern major river that defined Mesopotamia along with the Euphrates, which flows from Armenia into the Persian Gulf. He does not mention where on the long Tigris he was standing, but perhaps the significance is that he is not in the city of Babylon, which is on the Euphrates, but rather on the river that provides the border between Babylonia and Persia.

What he first sees is reminiscent (as is the reporting) of Ezekiel 1, where that prophet received an epiphany of God. Though Ezekiel devotes the majority of his description to the mighty cherubim who accompany God, he does describe God himself as "a figure like that of a man" looming above a throne of lapis lazuli. The figure itself from the waist up "looked like glowing metal, as if full of fire, and that from there down he looked like fire; and brilliant light surrounded him. Like the appearance of a rainbow in the clouds on a rainy day, so was the radiance around him" (Ezek 1:27-28). Ezekiel found himself prostrate since he realized that "this was the appearance of the likeness of the glory of the LORD" (Ezek 1:28).

The figure before Daniel is described in different terms but of equal magnificence. Also in appearance like a man, this figure was dressed in linen (the cloth worn by priests) held together by a belt of the finest gold from a region called Uphaz. His appearance, like that of the divine figure in Ezekiel, is described by reference to precious metals and gems as well as fire: "His body was like topaz, his face like lightning, his eyes like flaming torches, his arms and legs like the gleam of burnished bronze" (Dan 10:4-6). When this figure spoke, he sounded like a multitude of people speaking (Dan 10:6). In the book of Daniel, this figure represents God himself.

Ezekiel found himself on his face; so did Daniel. The experience of the appearance of God was so overwhelming that those who were with Daniel fled even though they did not see the vision. As for Daniel, when he was left alone, he found himself bereft of strength and collapsing into a deep sleep.

The next thing he knows (whether as he dreams or when he awakes) is that a hand is on him helping him to get up, first on his hands and knees and then eventually to stand up. In Ezekiel, it is God himself who helps the prophet up and speaks to him. Here it is another heavenly figure sent by God who does so and tells him that he intends to explain the significance of the vision. This heavenly messenger is never named, but it would not be stretching too far to imagine that this is Gabriel, whom we have encountered before as God's angelic messenger (Dan 8:16; 9:21). He will explain the vision to Daniel. In a departure from the first two visions (Daniel 7 and 8) . . . in which we get a description of the vision followed by the interpretation, we get the interpretation along with a recounting of the vision itself.

But first the messenger angel explains why it has taken three full weeks for him to respond to Daniel's plea for help, and his reasons provide an interesting window into late–Old Testament understanding of the spiritual world. Since it does further our understanding of the spiritual realm, we will take a bit of time to explore the angel's excuse for taking so long to come to Daniel.

The angel Gabriel. The angel—from now on we will assume it is Gabriel—tells Daniel that he responded immediately to Daniel's request for understanding his vision. After all, he tells Daniel that he is "highly esteemed" (Dan 10:11) and has humbled himself before God. Even with the good intention of coming right away, Gabriel admits that he was unable to do so. But why?

Gabriel says that he was blocked in his coming by "the prince of the Persian kingdom" (Dan 10:13). He was then detained "with the king of Persia" for three weeks. But then he was aided by Michael, "one of the chief princes" (Dan 10:13), and they won passage to finally come to meet Daniel.

There is nothing else quite like this in the Old Testament, so it is no wonder that readers today have difficulty with this verse. As with all enigmas in the Old Testament, it also leads some to read more than they should into the passage, so again we will spend some time with this scene and return to it in a later chapter to consider whether there is any relevance for us today.

As we work to understand this passage, we realize that, though it is unique in the Old Testament, there is a background to this scene. First, we need to realize, as would have been immediately obvious to the ancient readers, that all the characters in this drama are spiritual beings. We know that from the messenger who just arrived, Gabriel, and from Michael. Michael is called one of the chief princes but later is identified to Daniel as "your prince" (Dan 10:21).

That means that the prince of Persia is also a spiritual being, an angel, but since this angel is working against God's purposes, we would call this spiritual being a demon. Thus, we are in the realm of spiritual warfare. There is a battle among spiritual beings going on behind the scenes of the conflict between God's faithful people and those who seek to oppress them.

By the time the book of Daniel was written, God's people knew that there were angels but also spiritual powers who were working at counterpurposes to God. While no Old Testament person would have identified the serpent of Genesis 3:1 as the devil (the New Testament will make that specific identification; Rom 16:20; Rev 12:9), they would have recognized the serpent as a figurative representation of evil.[1] We do not get the story of a rebellion of spiritual beings against God anywhere in the Bible, but that is certainly implied by the fact that God called creation "very good" (Gen 1), and later spiritual beings try to undermine God's good intentions for creation.

We find another key background text to Daniel 10 in Moses' words found in Deuteronomy 32:7-9:

> Remember the days of old;
>> consider the generations long past.
> Ask your father and he will tell you,
>> your elders, and they will explain to you.
> When the Most High gave the nations their inheritance,
>> when he divided all mankind,
> he set up boundaries for the peoples
>> according to the number of the sons of God.[2]
> For the LORD's portion is his people,
>> Jacob his allotted inheritance.

Notice how verse 8 informs us that God divided humans into nations according to the number of the "sons of God," a phrase that we have seen most often means angels. This passage reflects Genesis 10, which describes seventy nations "each with its own language" (Gen 10:5, 20, 31). Genesis 10 ends with the statement, "These are the clans of Noah's sons, according to their lines of descent, within their nations. From these the nations spread out over the earth after the flood" (Gen 10:32).

Putting these passages together tells us that God assigned each nation their own angelic being. In Daniel 10, Michael is "your angel," the angel assigned to Israel, while the "prince of Persia" is the "son of God" assigned to Persia. This spiritual being is hostile toward God and his angels.

Now we can see that Gabriel's tardiness is the result of this spiritual battle. Michael, though, successfully fought his way through the spiritual forces supporting the nation of Persia, so that Gabriel can now "explain to you [Daniel] what will happen to your people in the future, for the vision concerns a time yet to come" (Dan 10:14).

Daniel responds to Gabriel by confessing his weakness and anguish. He is exhausted and overwhelmed by the situation and likely the foreboding of the vision. Gabriel, however, touches him and gives him the strength that he needs to hear the message.

Gabriel is determined to tell him what is to come since it is written in the Book of Truth. But after he does, he announces, he will have to return to the spiritual battle to fight the spirit prince of Persia and ultimately the spirit prince of Greece (anticipated by the goat of Dan 8). In this, only Michael, Israel's spirit prince, supports him.

PART ONE: VISION: THE KINGS OF THE
SOUTH AND THE NORTH (DAN 11:1-36)

Gabriel then explains the vision in a way that shows it looks into the future starting with the near present and extending as far as the end of history. The prophecy is described in the form of unnamed kings who will arise in power and who will vie with each other and also will oppress the people of God.

These nameless kings would be unknown to Daniel in the sixth century BC. However, to us living centuries later, we can give names to the various persons described in general terms in this chapter. Indeed, from our vantage point, the prophecy is so precise to actual history that many, particularly those who don't believe that God can reveal the future, argue that this is prophecy written after the fact, that it was written after all the events and put into the mouth of a sixth-century figure, Daniel, to give it the appearance of prophecy. The remarks of Sibley Towner, whom we mentioned earlier in chapter two, bear repeating for their brutal honestly in denying the possibility of divine revelation concerning such matters:

We need to assume that the vision as a whole is a prophecy after the fact. Why? Because human beings are unable accurately to predict future events centuries in advance and to say that Daniel could do so, even on the basis of a symbolic revelation vouchsafed to him by God and interpreted by an angel, is to fly in the face of the certainties of human nature. So what we have here is in fact not a road map of the future laid down in the sixth century B.C. but an interpretation of the events of the author's own time, 167–164 B.C.

While a natural conclusion for those who don't believe God can or is in the business of telling his prophets and seers anything about the future, Isaiah reminds us that it is precisely this attribute that differentiates the true God from the false gods. Indeed, the prophet Isaiah reports that God ridicules the worship of false gods because they are impotent in many ways, including their inability to know anything about the future. God mockingly addresses the false gods by saying:

> Tell us, you idols, what is going to happen.
> Tell us what the former things were,
>   so that we may consider them
>   and know their final outcome.
> Or declare to us the things to come,
>   tell us what the future holds,
>   so we may know that you are gods. (Is 41:22-23)

So it is precisely because God can do what Daniel 11 says he can do that differentiates him from the false gods. We should not be surprised at the precision of the prophetic foresight of Daniel 11 even while we are left with some questions of detail, particularly at the beginning and end of the chapter.

Daniel's vision describes the future as a series of kings who "will arise," vying with each other and replacing each other before giving way to yet another king who arises. This language of unnamed kings who "arise" is not unique in the book of Daniel and can be found in certain prophecy-like texts found written in the Akkadian language, most notably the Dynastic Prophecy.[3] This comparison should not be surprising since God's revelation uses forms that are familiar to its ancient cultural setting, but we should also beware of assuming that these comparable texts function the same way in these different cultures.

Section one: The transition from the Persian to the Greek Empire (Dan 11:1-4). According to Daniel 10, the seer receives this vision at the very beginning of the Persian period, during the reign of Cyrus the Great, who had just defeated Babylon and inherited its vast empire. Persia would dominate the Near East for the next couple of centuries, from approximately 539 to 331 BC. Thus, it is slightly perplexing when the prophecy begins, "Three more kings will arise in Persia, and then a fourth" (Dan 11:2), when we know that more than three kings succeeded Cyrus before the end of the Persian period.

Some scholars simply concede that the second-century-BC author of Daniel simply did not know any better and thus made a mistake. Those of us who do not hold this viewpoint propose different possible scenarios for what is going on here. Perhaps, as one scholar suggests, the four kings are those who follow Cyrus on the throne beginning with Smerdis, Cambyses, and Darius I, and that the rich fourth king is Xerxes, known from the book of Esther.[4] While Xerxes was far from the last king of Persia, he was the one who first campaigned against the Greeks and thus "stir[red] up everyone against the kingdom of Greece" (Dan 11:2). I find this highly plausible, but so is the possibility that here we have a numerical parallelism that is not uncommon in wisdom literature (see for instance, Prov 30:18-31) and the prophetic tradition. In the latter, we can take special note of the judgment oracles against the nations in Amos 1 and 2. These oracles each begin with such a numerical parallelism as it lays out the indictment against the various nations. The first oracle against Damascus is a case in point: "For three sins of Damascus, even for four, I will not relent" (Amos 1:3).

Notable is the fact that the passage goes on to simply give one example of a sin: "Because she threshed Gilead with sledges having iron teeth" (Amos 1:3). The "three, yea four" parallelism seems to have the effect of saying that there are a number of accusations to be made, not that there are specifically only three or four. So rather than thinking the "three, yea four" number of kings in Daniel means that there will be only four, it could be that a number of Persian kings will appear before the Greeks take over.

While there is some question about the part of the prophecy concerning Persia, no one doubts the accuracy of the prophetic depiction of what follows, at least until the very end. For some, Daniel just can't win though; either it's not accurate enough and therefore wrong, or it's too accurate and specific and therefore must be prophecy after the fact.

But in any case, the last mentioned Persian king is said to grow wealthy and provoke the Greeks. But this will prove a fatal mistake as a "mighty king" will come to power among the Greeks "who will rule with great power and do as he pleases" (Dan 11:3). Daniel 8 speaks of this transition in the language of a battle between the ram and the victorious goat and clearly refers to Alexander the Great's sweeping victory and incorporation of the Persian Empire after his defeat of Darius III at the Battle of Gaugamela in 331 BC.

As impressive as Alexander's life and conquest were, the prophecy only devotes a verse to him before moving on to his aftermath. After all, we know Alexander himself did not long survive his victory, and after his death we know his empire was "parceled out toward the four winds of heaven." It did not go to his descendants but rather was divided between his four most powerful generals, who established power bases in Thrace and Asia Minor, Macedonia and Greece, Antioch in Syria, and in Alexandria in Egypt. At this point the prophecy turns its attention to the last two of these kingdoms.

Section two: Back and forth between the Kings of the South and the North (Dan 11:5-20). The largest part of this final prophecy charts the interaction between kings of the South and kings of the North. From our historical vantage point it is immediately obvious that these refer to two of the kingdoms established by Alexander's successors and their descendants, stretching from the last part of the fourth century to the middle of the second century BC.

The first king of the North is Seleucus, who established his capital at Antioch in Syria, and the first king of the South is Ptolemy, who established his capital at Alexandria in Egypt. Thus, we commonly refer to the dynasties that flow from them as the Seleucids and the Ptolemies and their kingdoms as the Seleucid and Ptolemaic kingdoms.

Before beginning to rehearse the interactions between these kingdoms as prophetically described in Daniel 11, we should take note of the unfortunate location of Jerusalem as right in the middle between these two kingdoms. We will find that Jerusalem and the province of Yehud are contended territory between these two kingdoms as they jockey with each other for power.

As we move into this phase of the prophecy, we can, in historical retrospect, plug in names for the various kings and others in the North and the South. Indeed, it is as simple as reading a historical account of the period written by a modern historian who is basing their research on the writings of ancient historians. In other words, a modern reader not versed in the history of the eastern Mediterranean region, including Egypt in the late fourth to mid-second century BC, will be mystified by Daniel 11:5-45, but those who are familiar with the time period will recognize well-known monarchs and their actions in these words. That said, we will run into a well-known and difficult reference in regard to the final king in the very end of this section. Indeed, it is this final king who seems to be the focus of the whole section, though the question will be, Does the comment on the final king morph into something larger and further in the future?

What is clear is that the time period between the fall of Persia to Greece and the early Greek period is simply creating the setting for sustained focus on the climactic king. Thus, as we describe the contents of Daniel 11:5-20 and make reference to the history it points to (from our historical vantage point), we will not be exhaustive.[5] To make things clear, I will summarize the contents of the biblical text in normal font but italicize our later understanding in the light of historical events.

The first round (Dan 11:5-6) of the kings of the South (Ptolemaic) and the North (Seleucid) describes how the first king of the former will grow in power, but he will have a commander who grows even more powerful. *Here the reference is to the first Ptolemaic king, Ptolemy I, and* his commander, *Seleucus I, who had gone to Egypt in the midst of a conflict with another general of the deceased Alexander—namely, Antiochus.* But the king and his commander eventually form an alliance. *Ptolemy and Seleucus together defeated Antiochus and soon after established the latter's kingdom with its capital at Antioch. Palestine with its major city at Jerusalem was supposed be part of the Seleucid kingdom, but Ptolemy took it. Seleucus and his successors never conceded this, and thus conflict would break out over the long run between the two dynasties.* The daughter of the king of the South will try to form an alliance with the North but fail. *Berenice, the daughter of Ptolemy II Philadelphus, a member of the royal family, was given in marriage to a grandson of Seleucus in an attempt at a dynastic marriage between the two sides. The grandson had been divorced from his first wife, Laodice, who eventually reconciled with her former husband but then assassinated him, Berenice, and her son.* Thus, the daughter of the king of the South did not maintain her power.

In Daniel 11:7-10 we hear that a family member of the previously mentioned daughter of the king of the South came to the throne. *Berenice's brother, Ptolemy III Euergetes, took the throne in Alexandria around 246 BC. He warred against the new king of the North, Seleucus II Callinicus, the son of Laodice who had killed his sister.* He was successful, and in good Near Eastern practice (see comments above on Daniel 1:1-3), he took the idols and other ritual paraphernalia from Syria back to Egypt. But eventually the North attacked the South. While not victorious, the North recovered lost land.

Daniel 11:10 says that the son of the king of the North (*Seleucus II*)—namely, *Seleucus III Cerannus (227–223 BC), and especially Antichus III (223–187 BC) swept into the South as far as the fortress (maybe Gaza, south of Jerusalem).* But then the king of the South (*Ptolemy IV Philopater*), according to Daniel 11:11, fought the king of the North (*Antiochus III) in a battle that has come to be known as battle of Raphia (217 BC).* The king of the South won, but his victory was short-lived because the king of the North came back and pushed back against the South.

The king of the South then faces an uprising (Dan 11:14) *in the form of native Egyptians who rebelled against the foreign Greek leadership*. The next section (Dan 11:15-19) speaks of the growing power of the king of the North (*still Antiochus III*) but then his eventual failure (he "will stumble and fall, to be seen no more," Dan 11:19). The passage mentions his success in "the Beautiful Land," *Palestine, with its main city, Jerusalem* (*Dan 8:9; 11:41; cf. Jer 3:19*). He did give his daughter (*Cleopatra*) to the king of the South at the time (*Ptolemy V*) in another attempt at an alliance of sorts through a dynastic marriage. But this failed, since his daughter turned her loyalties and affections to the South ("his plans will not succeed or help him," Dan 11:17). *She became the major power in the South after her husband died, and when she died in 182, her son Ptolemy VI Philometer became king of the South eight years later.*

This section concludes (Dan 11:21) with the successor to the king of the North (*Seleucus IV; 187–175 BC*), whose reign comes to an end because of a tax collector (*Heliodorus*). *He dies around the time his younger brother, Antiochus IV, is freed from Rome, where he had been a hostage.*

Section three: A "contemptible person" (Dan 11:21-35). Attention now turns to a contemptible person, who has not been given "the honor of royalty" (*the aforementioned, Antiochus Epiphanes IV*). *We have already seen, particularly in Daniel 8, that this king proved to be particularly hostile to the Jewish people in the mid-second century BC. The timing of the release of Antiochus IV and the death of Seleucus IV are particularly suspicious because the latter's son replaced Antiochus IV as a hostage in Rome (thus not naturally of royalty).*

This person will invade the kingdom and destroy an overwhelming army (*perhaps a reference to Antiochus's taking the Seleucid kingdom?*) and a "prince of the covenant will be destroyed" (*perhaps a dischronologized reference to the deposing of the high priest Onias III; Dan 11:22*) through intrigue. He then will reach an agreement with him and invade the "richest provinces" (Dan 11:24) successfully and distribute the plunder.

Then he will come into conflict with the king of the South (*the young Ptolemaic ruler Ptolemy VI*), who will be betrayed by his close confidants ("those who eat from the king's provisions", Dan 11:26; *Eulaeus and Lenaeus, who initiated an anti-Seleucid policy*). The two kings (*Antiochus IV and Ptolemy VI; or this could possibly be a reference to the fact that Ptolemy VI and his brother Ptolemy VII had a falling out, each declaring themselves king*) will then lie to each other, but nothing will happen except the king of the North will return to his country with wealth but also anger at the "holy covenant" (*God's people who live around Jerusalem*; Dan 11:28).

After a while he (*Antiochus IV*) will try to invade the South again (*after the two Ptolemy brothers reconciled*) but this time with absolutely no success since he will be opposed by "ships of the western coastlands" (Dan 11:30; *he was confronted by the Roman legate Popillius Laenas with a senate mandate that he withdraw*). And again, he will vent his frustration against the holy covenant but show favor to those who abandon that covenant.

The practical result of this is that he will "desecrate the temple fortress and will abolish the daily sacrifice" (*Antiochus shut down the* tamid, *the sacrifices that the priests offered every evening and morning at the temple*) and "set up the abomination that causes desolation" (Dan 11:31; *he placed a meteorite dedicated to Baal Shamen, the Syrian version of the Greek god Zeus, in the temple*). There will be those who violate the covenant at his instigation (*the pro-Hellenistic Jewish party; the priest Menelaus*), but there will be resistance from "the people who know their God" (Dan 11:32). The latter may be the same as the "wise" (Dan 11:33), who will instruct many but themselves suffer persecution. This persecution is likened to a refining that will cease at the end, which has an "appointed time" (Dan 11:35).

PART TWO: THE KING WHO DOES AS HE PLEASES (DAN 11:36-45)

We have no indication in the text that we have moved on from Antiochus IV to another king. However, as the passage continues, this king takes on larger-than-life dimensions—even, as Richard Clifford points out, mythological dimensions.[6] The complication for our reading is that, while Daniel 11:36-39 remains a reasonable anticipation of the historical Antiochus IV, Daniel 11:40-45 does not conform to what we know about the end of Antiochus's life. These verses describe the king of the North attacking the king of the South and in the process taking the Beautiful Land, which we have already seen is a reference to Palestine with its capital in Jerusalem. But as far as we know, Antiochus IV did not "extend his power over many countries; Egypt will not escape" (Dan 11:42). And further, he did not die when he pitched his tent between "the seas at the beautiful holy mountain" (Dan 11:45).

As we observed in chapter two, some respond to this anomaly by saying that up to this point in Daniel 11 we have a prophecy after the fact, written by an anonymous author living during the reign of Antiochus IV in the midst of that king's persecution of the people of God. But now at the end, we have an attempt at real prophecy—that fails. Again, from what we know, Antiochus neither successfully sweeps through the nations, and he certainly does not take Egypt. He also does not die in the way Daniel 11:45 implies.

What are we to make of this if we do believe this chapter contains actual prophecy? We have a clue at the beginning of Daniel 11:40 that what follows takes place "at the time of the end." In addition, we will see that Daniel 12:1-4 describes the revivification of the dead, "some to everlasting life, others to shame and everlasting contempt" (Dan 12:2). Thus a number of scholars believe that the horrific Antiochus IV becomes a type of a wicked figure at the end of history (in the New Testament referred to as the antichrist) who will be defeated by God.

PART THREE: "SOME TO EVERLASTING LIFE, OTHERS TO SHAME" (DAN 12:1-4)

Daniel's final vision does not end with chapter 11 and the demise of the "king [who] will do as he pleases" (Dan 11:36) but goes on to describe the aftermath, which takes us further into the future with more detail than any other passage in the Old Testament.

Gabriel, the messenger angel, announces, "at that time," after the death of that final enemy of God's people (see previous section), the angel Michael will arise. We have already met Michael in the narrative introduction to the vision as the angel who is Israel's "prince" and the one who fought against the prince of Persia to get Gabriel to Daniel. Here our understanding of Michael is supported, as he is described as the "great prince who protects your [Daniel's] people" (Dan 12:1).

Michael's appearance implies conflict between God's spiritual forces and those forces that are ranged against God. This battle lies behind the "time of distress" (Dan 12:1). Gabriel tells Daniel that this conflict will be unprecedented, though not much more is said about the conflict except the good news that Daniel's people, "everyone whose name is found written in the book—will be delivered" (also 11:1).

Here we are led to ask, Who are these people? And what is the book? In the ancient Near East, there was a conception of the Tablet of Destiny, a book that spells out the future. In the Bible, there is also a mention of a book or books that anticipate the future, recording those who will find deliverance from the final conflict. These people are Daniel's people. Israel, yes, but more likely the faithful among Israel. Momentarily, these people will be called "those who are wise" (Dan 12:3), in Hebrew the *maskilim*, the ones who have insight, who are faithful in spite of the persecution.

But what is that deliverance? It is here that we learn more about the afterlife than any other place in the Old Testament. Though there are hints elsewhere, indeed, Daniel 12:2-3 is the only place that boldly speaks of the dead rising up to one of two fates.

Multitudes, Gabriel says, will rise from the dust of the earth. Their sleep in the dust, a euphemism for death, will come to an end, and they will either awake to everlasting life or to shame and everlasting contempt. In other words, they will all have everlasting life, but some will have life in the fullness of that term, while others will not.

It is the *maskilim* who are wise and have taught wisdom and righteousness to others who will have everlasting life described in the most promising terms as shining in the brightness of the heavens like the stars forever (Dan 12:3). While contrasting with the negative fate of all others, the vision lays out the promise of a glorious eternity to those who stay faithful in the midst of the present conflict.

Gabriel ends his speech with a curious exhortation given to Daniel. "But you, Daniel, roll up and seal the words of the scroll until the time of the end. Many will go here and there to increase knowledge" (Dan 12:4). After this marvelous vision, the interpreting angel does not tell Daniel to go out and proclaim it from the rooftops but rather to roll the document up and seal it. It has to do with the end, and as we will see in the next section, Daniel (and presumably those on his side of the divide) are to go on living in the present, not in the future. But to know that the future will bring victory also brings encouragement and strength for living in a difficult present.

In that light, it is difficult to understand whether the angel is positive about the many who "go here and there to increase knowledge" (Dan 12:4), but seeking knowledge or wisdom is not always a good thing, particularly when it involves human efforts apart from God. We only have to think of Adam and Eve and the tree of the knowledge of good and evil (Gen 3). Or the efforts of Job and his friends as they supply their own inadequate human knowledge. Here Gabriel has just imparted knowledge about the vision that looks to the end and then tells Daniel not to study it, to derive deeper insight or more detail about the end, but to roll it up and seal it. In other words, you know what you need to know to live in a difficult world with faith. Don't obsess about it, and get on living your faithful life until the end.

CONCLUSION

Again, we learn that, in spite of present difficulties, God is in control, and he will have the final victory. Throughout the era covered by this prophecy and especially at the end with the king who exalts himself, it looks like evil human power is in control. But no—"He will come to his end, and no one will help him" (Dan 11:45). God is in control, and "everyone whose name is found written in the book—will be delivered" (Dan 12:1).

DISCUSSION QUESTIONS

1. Some believe that the prophecies of Daniel 11 are so specific that they must be written after the events that they "predict." What are your thoughts about this? Can God use prophecy after the fact?

2. Gabriel tells Daniel that he and Michael were in a struggle with the spirit prince of Persia and will be in a struggle with the spirit prince of Greece. What do you make of this? Do you ever feel like you are in a struggle with evil spiritual forces?

3. Does this fourth vision that has come to Daniel encourage you or depress you? Why?

FOURTEEN

"Go Your Way till the End"

Daniel 12:5-13

We have worked our way now through the body of the book of Daniel, six stories of Daniel in a foreign court and four apocalyptic visions. Each story and vision in their own way spoke to the common theme of the book: in spite of present difficulties, God is in control, and he will have the final victory. The intended addressees are the *maskilim*, the wise or insightful ones, those who were faithful to God in the midst of the pressures and even persecution of cultures toxic to their faith. How encouraging these stories (chaps. 1–6) and visions (chaps. 7–12) would be to these faithful followers of God as they heard of Daniel's surviving, even thriving, in such a context. How encouraging it would have been for them to become aware of Daniel's visions (chaps. 7–12) that communicated to them the ultimate victory of God over the most horrific and powerful evil forces.

The stories are told and the visions are over. We turn now to the brief but significant final interchange between Daniel and his heavenly guides, which concludes the book.

THE FINAL SCENE (DAN 12:5-13)

This final scene follows fast on the conclusion of the vision, and its interpretation given in Daniel 11:1–12:4 while Daniel is still at the

Tigris River. There are two figures, one on each side of the river. One of them, presumably Gabriel, said to the other, "How long will it be before these astonishing things are fulfilled?" (Dan 12:6).

The other figure responds, but before we examine his response, we should make it clear who he is. He is described as "clothed in linen" (Dan 12:7), which links him back to the heavenly figure in Daniel 9:5, who we determined was none other than God himself. This identification is confirmed by the fact that he was standing "above the waters," since God is frequently depicted in Scripture as the one who controls and dominates the waters (Ps 29:3, 10; 77:16; 93:4).

Thus, we are to understand that it is Gabriel who is asking God "how long" must they endure the oppression before God has his final victory. The figure representing God then raises his right and his left hand before giving an answer. Typically when someone makes a vow to tell the truth they raise their right hand, but here God raises both to double down on the gesture. He also swears by himself since that is how we should understand the phrase "him who lives forever" (Dan 12:7).

God then answers: "It will be for a time, times [literally, 'two times'] and half a time" (Dan 12:7). We have seen this phrase before (Dan 7:25). Like there, this answer does not give the reader the type of information needed to plot an end on a calendar. Rather the answer demonstrates that there is a determined time of the end. While it looks like evil will have control forever, its dominance moves from a single time, to double time, but then time slows to half a time and finally stops. That said, while communicating that there is a determined end, this passage does not allow one to know whether the end will come in months, years, centuries, or millennia.

After hearing this, Daniel is not satisfied with the answer and prods further: "My lord, what will the outcome of all this be?" (Dan 12:8), but he is rebuffed even while more detail is given. "Go about your business, Daniel" is the gist of what he hears from the divine figure. The scroll (that represents the playing out of history) is set (rolled and sealed up). During the interval the wicked will still be wicked, but there will be many who "will be purified, made spotless and refined" (Dan 12:10). The wicked will not understand that God is in control and will have the final victory, but those who are wise (the faithful) will.

Then God throws in a final comment, this time about the length of time that the daily sacrifice, the *tamid*, when the priests offer sacrifices on behalf of the people in the morning and the evening, and the abomination of desolation (something that profanes the holy place) is set up. There will be 1,290 days. But then enigmatically he pronounces blessing on those who make it not just for the 1,290 days but for 1,335 days. This is indeed difficult for us to understand, but as we have commented before on the use of numbers in the book of Daniel, they are intentionally ambiguous. They give a sense that there is an endpoint but not the detail or precision to determine when on a calendar that endpoint will come.

But what is clear is that God again urges Daniel to, in effect, go about his regular life in spite of the fact that he has been made aware of great events that will happen in the future. This knowledge should not get him to change his life but rather to continue his daily work in the knowledge that God will have the victory over evil and that Daniel himself will "rise to receive" his "allotted inheritance" (Dan 12:13), surely a reference to the fact that he, like the other wise, will awake to everlasting life and "shine like the brightness of the heavens" (Dan 12:3).

CONCLUSION

After six stories and four visions that have repeatedly assured the reader that in spite of present difficulties, God is in control, and he will have the final victory, the book ends with the angelic interpreter telling Daniel to "go your way till the end" (Dan 12:13). In addressing Daniel the angel addresses us, the readers. Rest assured, the story of your life is in God's hands, and "you will rise to receive your allotted inheritance" (Dan 12:13). Don't fret about when this will happen; live in the light that it most certainly will.

DISCUSSION QUESTIONS

1. The six stories and four apocalyptic visions have come to a close. What overall purpose does this short conclusion to the book serve?

2. The angel tells Daniel that he should go about his business in spite of his dramatic experiences and visions. Do these words have any implications for your life today? How should you think and act in the light of what you read in the book of Daniel?

PART 3

Reading Daniel as a Twenty-First-Century Christian

When first encountered, Daniel can appear as a book that is vastly distant from the interests and concerns of Christians living in the twenty-first century AD, particularly those of us who live in the West. In this present section, I will be focusing on the meaning of the book of Daniel for twenty-first-century Western Christians for two reasons. First, it is the world in which I live in and that I know. Second, since this book is written in English, the West will be its primary audience, particularly the English-speaking West. That said, I will not reserve my comments totally to that world. I will respectfully and humbly speak about the global church, again for two primary reasons. First, those of us in the West always need to keep in mind our brothers and sisters around the world. We must do that without being patronizing. Indeed, my comments on the global church will not be for giving advice but more for the purpose of reminding the Western church that our experience is not universal. Regarding many topics, we in the West wrongly believe our experience is *the* human experience. Second, I will also bring to mind the global church knowing that previous books in this series have been translated from English into other languages, like Spanish, Portuguese, Thai, Korean, Chinese, and even

Finnish. What do the stories of a Judean man, Daniel, and his three friends living in an ancient foreign court have to say to us today? What do the strikingly bizarre visions of the future that Daniel experienced tell us today?

Hopefully, our study of the book of Daniel in the previous chapters has made the message clear to all of us, particularly as we have explored its central themes. In spite of present circumstances, God is in control, and he will have the final victory. We can see how that message met a dire need at the time that the book was written, but what about now? The same can be asked about the subsidiary theme: "You, faithful follower of God, like Daniel and his friends, can survive and even thrive in an atmosphere of persecution." But what does that message have to say to us who live in the prosperous and relatively calm societies of the Western world in the twenty-first century? In what follows, we will see that the book can contribute quite a lot to how we should live as faithful Christians in the midst of societies that are toxic (and in some societies that are outright hostile) to our faith.

Before we dive in, though, it is necessary to point out a frequent misuse of the book of Daniel, especially its second part. While the book of Daniel does intend to inform its readers about the exciting news that God will intervene at the end to rescue his people and to punish their oppressors, it does not have interest in giving us any information that will allow us to predict when that great event will happen.

I feel it is important to be clear about this because the books of Daniel and Revelation, along with other apocalyptic portions of the Bible (such as the "little apocalypses" of the Gospels; Mark 13 and parallels), have been misunderstood and misused in precisely this way. In the previous chapters, we have commented on the various numbers that are given in the book of Daniel, and we have observed that these numbers are not given to tell us a specific future date for the return of God, only to say to readers that there is a set time for that final day.

Daniel's message of hope to the beleaguered, faithful followers of God was not and is not to tell them that God was coming back at a particular date in time but simply that he was coming back and to live faithfully in the meantime. But that does not stop certain popular writers who prey on the anxieties of others to give them a false assurance that God will bring history to a close in the near future or on a particular date using apocalyptic material. Perhaps among the most notable examples in the Western evangelical church during my lifetime includes Hal Lindsey's best-selling book *The Late Great Planet Earth*, which was written in 1970 and, without naming a specific date, suggested that the biblical prophecies of Daniel and Revelation would come to pass in the next decade.[1] This book sold millions and millions of copies, making it the best-selling book ever in English at that time.

Another notable example, adopting a slightly different but equally faulty interpretation, was that provided by Harold Camping, who used not only the material from biblical apocalyptic literature but many other portions of Scripture to say that Jesus was going to return and fulfill the biblical expectation that God would come to save his people in September 1994.[2] He believed that Daniel 12:4 indicated that no one would be able to understand the message of Daniel until the end of time ("But you, Daniel, roll up and seal the words of the scroll until the time of the end"). He believed that he himself, living at the time just before the end, was one who "increase[d] knowledge," which he took positively as a reference to someone who at the end would actually understand the timing of the end. When Jesus did not come in September 1994 as he had argued, he likened himself to the prophet Jonah, who had predicted the destruction of Nineveh in forty days, a destruction that did not happen because God in his mercy decided to give pagans more time to repent. He then used the same biblical material later to say that Jesus would return in September 2011. When that failed to materialize, he repented, but only after many people had harmed their lives in significant ways financially and relationally, not to mention having their faith shaken.

These are just two notable, slightly different examples of a misuse of the apocalyptic material in Daniel. But actually there are hundreds of other less well-known or infamous examples all around the world. At the present time in the Western church, there is not a major influential figure like Hal Lindsey or Harold Camping, but there are lesser-known people in more local settings making similar cases. And it is just a matter of time before another self-understood end-time preacher rises up and convinces the unwary.

During the first Gulf War, two notable books were written by faculty members at Dallas Theological Seminary that gave the suggestion that the events in the Middle East at that time were lining up with biblical expectations of Christ's return, again using material from Daniel and Revelation.[3] Apparently these books sold hundreds of thousands of copies very quickly. When the war ended, sales abruptly stopped.

Why am I mentioning this here? As we move to a discussion of the continuing relevance of the book of Daniel today, many will think that such an approach is the way in which Daniel has continuing relevance. It is important, to state it again, to say that Daniel, while giving us the good news that God will come again (see below), is not telling us when. To rehearse a few of the most notable examples of this kind of misuse and remind us of the many, many other times around the world this biblical material has been so abused should inoculate us against what will surely be future attempts to misuse Daniel and other similar portions of Scripture.

Perhaps the saddest consequence of the obsession with Daniel as a tool to construct an apocalyptic timetable is that we often miss the important message that the book has for us today in the twenty-first century. It is to that message that we now turn.

FIFTEEN

How to Live in a Toxic Culture

Daniel 1–6

W hat do the stories in Daniel 1–6 tell us about living in a Western society as a Christian? We begin with this question because, as just stated, I and most of my readers live in a Western society. Of course, even within a Western society, there are differences. As I write this paragraph, I happen to have just finished a month-long lecture tour in New Zealand and Australia. While there are many similarities with the American society in which I grew up and live, there are differences. There are, for example, fewer Christians in proportion to the broader population here than in the States. In New Zealand and Australia, therefore, there is no illusion about being a Christian society. That said, I also travel around the United States as I teach the Bible, and there is an incredible diversity even within our country. Being a Christian in New York City feels different and raises different issues than being a Christian, say, in Birmingham, Alabama. Still I believe that the book of Daniel has an important message for us wherever we live. That's true even in non-Western societies, from Tokyo to Mumbai to Amman to Kampala to Montevideo. I will have a word to say about this in a bit. But we begin with a review and further explication of the stories in Daniel that will provide the backdrop for our comments about their implications for how we live today.

"GO THOU AND DO LIKEWISE": READING DANIEL FOR LIFE WISDOM

Before doing that, however, a few words about the legitimacy of reading the book of Daniel for life lessons. While many readers read Old Testament and New Testament stories for moral guidance, others raise cautions about this practice. Some of these cautions are legitimate, but it goes too far to say that the biblical stories, including those in Daniel, don't intend to teach us how to live.

The cautions are particularly appropriate when it comes to the Old Testament. After all, we do live in the period after Christ has come, and his coming has had a tremendous effect on how we read the Old Testament. For instance, in the Old Testament, we read about the offering of sacrifices, God's people engaging in warfare against their enemies, the prohibition of eating certain foods, and so forth. Christ's coming means that we don't offer sacrifices since he has offered himself as the once-and-for-all sacrifice (Heb 10:1-18). Also, we do not engage in physical battles like those in the Old Testament but rather in spiritual battles (see chap. 16), and we can eat all foods because the food laws, which intended to keep Israelites separate from Gentiles, are no longer relevant since Christ has caused the "wall of hostility" between the two to come down (Eph 2:14-18).

But, on the other hand, we also read that Jesus taught:

Do not think that I have come to abolish the Law or the Prophets; I have not come to abolish them but to fulfill them. For truly I tell you, until heaven and earth disappear, not the smallest letter, not the least stroke of a pen, will by any means disappear from the Law until everything is accomplished. Therefore anyone who sets aside one of the least of these commands and teaches others accordingly will be called least in the kingdom of heaven, but whoever practices and teaches these commands will be called great in the kingdom of heaven. For I tell you that unless your righteousness surpasses that of the Pharisees and the teachers of the law, you will certainly not enter the kingdom of heaven. (Mt 5:17-20)

This passage and others tell us that while a number of matters have been fulfilled by Christ and thus are no longer relevant for the Christian life, many other matters of the Law and the Prophets are still instructive to Christians who want to seek a life pleasing to the God who saved them.

The Old Testament narratives will often offer illustrations of attitudes and behaviors that either show obedience or disobedience to God's will for our lives, and so can provide us with life lessons for today (1 Cor 10:1-10). We just have to be careful to take into account the discontinuity as well as the continuity between the two Testaments. We also have to make a distinction between characters demonstrating obedience to law as opposed to examples of a biblical character acting foolishly or wisely in their contexts. In the latter case, we may get a principle for how to live, but then we will need to ask the question of wisdom: How do we implement this principle in our lives in our particular context?

Finally, I will simply point out that the book of Daniel was written in large measure for the express purpose of being a guide to God's people who live in the midst of a troubled world, particularly one that is toxic to our faith. The contents of the book indicate that it was written about a time period of persecution, likely by a person who lived in that or a similar time. The purpose was to give comfort to people who lived when evil had a grip on the world in order to remind them that, in spite of present difficulties, God was in control, and he will have the final victory. That message resonates through the ages down to the present day. Further, the narratives give us guidance about how to live in a difficult world not only to survive but to thrive. Let's look at the specific teaching of the first half of Daniel to see how this works out.

HOW TO NAVIGATE AND EVEN THRIVE IN A TOXIC CULTURE (DANIEL 1 AND 2)

In our exposition of Daniel 1 and 2, we observed Daniel and his three friends being forced to move from Judah, the heartland of their faith, to the hostile environment of Babylon. They were no longer free to practice their devotion to Yahweh in the way that they wanted but were compelled to shape their lives in a way that pleased their captors.

They had their names changed from names that praised the true God to those that praised the false gods of the Babylonians. They may even have been castrated as those who served in the Babylonian court were. This would have been problematic not only for their personal lives but for their religious sensibilities (Lev 21:20). Perhaps most troubling to these devout young men, they were subjected to an educational curriculum that would have been toxic to their faith and even subjected to a diet that had the intention of making their bodies suitable for service in the court.

What is interesting is that the narrative implies that they did not protest most of these impositions but rather endured them. The one exception we saw had to do with the food, and surprisingly it does not appear that their protest had to do with a specifically religious obligation but rather served to give God room to work in their lives. Their physique was robust in spite of their diet of water and vegetables, showing that it was God who made them that way, not the rich food and wine of Nebuchadnezzar. And even here their protest was private. No one knew that they were eating food not authorized by the court except them and the person who delivered the food, whose own life would have been in jeopardy if their refusal to eat the palace's food became known.

Can we learn anything today, living in the twenty-first century, from the actions of Daniel and his three friends? I believe so, though we must acknowledge the differences between our situation and that of God's people in the sixth century BC.

As mentioned above, I will initially focus my comments on the situation in the part of the contemporary world in which I live—namely, the twenty-first-century West, particularly America. The differences between Daniel's situation and ours is dramatic. Daniel and his three friends were thrust against their will into a pagan culture, and they were being forced to conform their own beliefs to those around them. We live in a culture that grants the right to worship or not as one sees fit. No one compels us to worship false deities or forbids us from worshiping in the way that we want. Indeed, today's Western world for the most part grants us historically unprecedented freedom of religion.

That said, people of faith should not deceive themselves into thinking that we live in a toxic-free environment. We face challenges and protests to our beliefs every day. Our culture is not Christian nor religious. We live, as the New Testament would put it, "in the world."

We put ourselves in danger if we think that our culture is Christian or that it even should be Christian. The question should not be how can we make our culture Christian, but how should we as Christians, and corporately as a church, live in a world toxic to the faith?

Unfortunately, too many Christian leaders want to lead America back to Christian roots that never existed in the first place. That is not to say that we shouldn't advocate for values in our democratic society that reflect those of our faith, but we should steer clear of trying to force non-Christians to act like Christians. We should rather want to persuade them to become Christians themselves. As the great Welsh preacher Martyn Lloyd-Jones put it in a previous generation:

> The New Testament is never interested in conduct and behavior in itself. I can go further and say that the New Testament does not make an appeal for good behavior to anyone but to Christian people. The New Testament is not interested, as such, in the morality of the world. It tells us quite plainly that you can expect nothing from the world but sin, and that in its fallen condition it is incapable of anything else. In Titus 3:3 Paul tells us that we were all once like that: "For we ourselves were sometimes foolish, disobedient, deceived, serving divers lusts and pleasures, living in malice and envy, hateful, and hating one another." Thus there is nothing, according to the New Testament that is so fatuous and so utterly futile, as to turn to such people and appeal to them to live the Christian life. . . . The truth is that it only has one message for people like that—the message of repentance.[1]

In our American, democratic society, Christians should certainly advocate and try to persuade our fellow citizens concerning what we believe are values that are healthy for the society at large, including the sanctity of life in the womb and the promotion of a traditional view of marriage. But if the society at large opts to allow for abortion or same-sex marriage, should we in the first place expect anything else? And in the second place, should we respond to society by publicly ranting and raving and disparaging the culture at-large, or should we work patiently and respectfully within our system of government and also on a personal level? We should care about our society's health, but our response should be primarily evangelistic rather than political. We can and should work in the realm of the political, but we should not act like God depends on our government acting like the church. Daniel is an example of someone who tolerated much that was toxic to his faith and still helped the pagan leaders when he could.

BEING WILLING TO DIE FOR YOUR FAITH (DAN 3)

The message of comfort in the midst of persecution is an important one that allows God's people to function in a hostile environment. We have seen that the book of Daniel does not give us a one-size-fits-all formula for how God's people interact with powerful forces that are not friendly to our religious values. Sometimes Daniel and the three friends withdraw (eating vegetables and drinking their water in private [Dan 1]) or praying not in the public square but in the privacy of their own rooms (Dan 6) or sometimes publicly protesting (not kneeling on the plains of Dura to the golden statue [Dan 3]). At other times, they try to persuade (Daniel urging Nebuchadnezzar to avoid attitudes and behaviors that would lead to his unhinging [Dan 4]), and on and on.

The one thing that is clear and consistent is that they do not go out of their way to offend the authorities that have the power of life and death over them. Their behavior is such that they do not feel that they have to die on every hill, but rather they will absorb a tremendous amount of hurt and disappointment rather than prod the beasts who are their oppressors.

But that said, they will not betray their faith. They were willing to die rather than deny their faith. While Daniel in the lions' den demonstrates this point (Dan 6), we see this most dramatically in Daniel 3, when the three friends refuse to bow to Nebuchadnezzar's golden statue. Even here, they don't make a big, public display of their refusal. Nebuchadnezzar does not notice, but their jealous peers make a point of outing them.

They then were brought into Nebuchadnezzar's presence in order to rectify their aberrant behavior but this time under specific threat to their lives from the king: "But if you do not worship it, you will be thrown immediately into a blazing furnace" (Dan 3:15). They respond with great courage:

> King Nebuchadnezzar, we do not need to defend ourselves before you in this matter. If we are thrown into the blazing furnace, the God we serve is able to deliver us from it, and he will deliver us from Your Majesty's hand. But even if he does not, we want you to know, Your Majesty, that we will not serve your gods or worship the image of gold you have set up. (Dan 3:16-18)

We sometimes are so rightly impressed by God's rescue of the three friends from the blazing furnace that we forget their willingness, and the real possibility, that they may die. We see this in their statement, "But even if he does not" rescue us. There is no promise in the book of Daniel or anywhere in Scripture that God will keep his people from death. God will have the victory in the end, but in the meantime we might be called to give up our lives rather than deny the faith.

Certainly that was the case in the early church, even during New Testament times. All we have to do is think of Stephen who, because of his testimony concerning Jesus, was accused of seeking "blasphemous words against Moses and against God" (Acts 6:11). When asked if the charge was true by the high priest, Stephen rehearsed the history of God's redemption of his people starting with Abraham. Rather than cowering in fear or denying his faith, he ended by calling out: "Look, . . . I see heaven open and the Son of Man standing at the right hand of God" (Acts 7:56). In this he knew he was emulating his Lord, to whom he called out while they were stoning him to death: "Lord Jesus, receive my spirit. . . . Lord, do not hold this sin against them" (Acts 7:59-60).

This call to martyrdom seems far from our experience in the Western church. And we should thank God it is. When we think of what are really minor slights and insults that Christians in America sometimes experience, we should remember those who are called to experience much worse than we must.

Again, we should thank God that the call to martyrdom is far from our experience (for now), but as we do so, we should not forget that our brothers and sisters around the world face the same kind of decision that Daniel and his three friends did in the face of a government or a culture that would harm them, even kill them, for their faith. The reality of martyrdom is not a thing of the past but a very present reality. While working as much as we can to help our brothers and sisters in those parts of the world where people are dying for their faith, we should pray for them that they stand firm in their commitment to Jesus.

CONFRONTING THE POWERS OF
THE WORLD (DAN 4 AND 5)

At first, readers may be stunned by how compliant Daniel and the three friends are to the various Babylonian and Persian powers who force them to serve as wise men. After all, Babylon and specifically Nebuchadnezzar destroyed Jerusalem and deported its leading citizens. Daniel and his three friends were in the first wave of deportations (605 BC) before the destruction (587 BC). The Persians inherited Judah as a province when they defeated Babylon (539 BC), while Daniel at least was still alive and active in the court.

For the most part, Daniel and the other men serve the interests of the empire that oppressed them and their people. Perhaps they do so with the knowledge that God is in control and will have the final victory and that their present plight is connected to the covenant disobedience of God's people (as Daniel expresses in his prayer in Dan 9). We have seen above (see How to Navigate and Even Thrive in a Toxic Culture) how Daniel and his friends live life in a way that avoids censure and leads to success but that they do so without compromising their faith in a fundamental way. They are willing to die if necessary for their faith (see Being Willing to Die for Your Faith). But now we pause to see that when the situation calls for it, they are also willing to confront the powers.

When the four men refuse to eat the food mandated by the king, they resisted the coercion of the empire early on, but this resistance was a private affair. In Daniel 2, Daniel informs Nebuchadnezzar of the content of the dream and interprets it, thus avoiding the death penalty that the king imposed on all the wise men of the kingdom. Interestingly, Calvin felt like he had to justify why Daniel responded so quickly and did not allow the king to kill more pagan wise men.[2] The interpretation of the dream, however, is subversive of empire, Nebuchadnezzar's and the ones that would follow, because it pictures the ultimate victory of God over them. The story of Daniel 3 (the three friends' refusal to bow to the statue of gold) is also subversive to the desires of the emperor as is Daniel's refusal to stop praying in response to Darius's decree (Dan 6).

Daniel 4 is the story of Nebuchadnezzar's madness. Here we see Daniel interpreting yet another royal dream. In this one, the dream and its interpretation challenges Nebuchadnezzar's pride. But it is especially in Daniel 5 that we see resistance to pagan rule as the latter manifests itself, the blasphemous toasting of false gods using the sacred utensils of the temple. Here Daniel expresses himself in an openly disdainful tone to the powerful Babylonian ruler.

CONCLUSION

In this chapter we have highlighted three major themes found in the first six chapters of Daniel that I believe the author is highlighting so that later readers might learn to apply them to their lives. First of all, we see Daniel and the three friends navigating life in a culture toxic to their faith. We see that they are not to apply a single one-size-fits-all situations principle (withdraw, attack, transform, etc.), but they use their wisdom to react in a way that allows them to remain faithful and even succeed in their difficult circumstances. Second, we also learn that in rare circumstances, when it becomes a choice of life or their fundamental relationship with God, they will choose the latter. And then, third, even though the four men do not adopt a lifestyle of resistance and protest, at the right time, they are willing to challenge the powers that be.

DISCUSSION QUESTIONS

1. Think about the culture you live in. In what way is it toxic to your faith?

2. How does the book of Daniel help you to think about how you should navigate the culture in which you live?

3. Where do you think it is appropriate for Christians to stand up to the toxic powers of your culture?

4. As you read about the three friends of Daniel standing up to Nebuchadnezzar even with the threat of death, does that frighten you or encourage you in your faith? Why?

SIXTEEN

Finding Comfort in God's Ultimate Victory

Daniel 7–12

I n a word, Daniel 7–12 expresses a bold expectation of a future divine intervention against those who resist God and persecute his people. They will be judged while his people will be saved. Daniel 12:1-3 gives this message an eternal perspective when it announces, more clearly than anywhere else in the Old Testament, that there will be a final reckoning that will clearly divide those who are faithful to God from those who are not:

> At that time Michael, the great prince who protects your people, will arise. There will be a time of distress such as has not happened from the beginning of nations until then. But at that time your people—everyone whose name is found written in the book—will be delivered. Multitudes who sleep in the dust of the earth will awake: some to everlasting life, others to shame and everlasting contempt. Those who are wise will shine like the brightness of the heavens, and those who lead many to righteousness, like the stars for ever and ever. (Dan 12:1-3)

So what message should those of us living in the twenty-first century take from Daniel 7–12? We answer this question in the light of the further revelation of the New Testament, but we do so by providing more background in the Old Testament.

Daniel 7–12 fits into the broader biblical drama of God's fight against evil. As I have explained elsewhere, this drama has five phases, and as we will see, Daniel fits into phase three.[1]

PHASE ONE: GOD FIGHTS ISRAEL'S FLESH-AND-BLOOD ENEMIES

Genesis 1–2 informs the reader that God created the cosmos, the earth, and his human creatures, and when he was finished the narrator tells us, "God saw all that he had made, and it was very good" (Gen 1:31). There is no hint of conflict in God's good creation. The man and the woman live in harmony with each other ("Adam and his wife were both naked, and they felt no shame," Gen 2:25) in the world.

Nonetheless, there is the hint of trouble in God's charge to the man to guard the garden (Gen 2:15), a responsibility that is shown to be relevant when a hostile force, the serpent, makes a sudden appearance speaking at cross-purposes with God's intention for his human creatures (Gen 3:1).[2] When the serpent makes his appearance, Adam and Eve fail miserably to guard the garden by choosing not to obey God but rather to assert their moral autonomy as they eat the forbidden fruit from the tree of the knowledge of good and evil. The result is their ejection from Eden and the introduction of conflict most communicated pointedly by the punishment levied on the serpent: "And I will put enmity between you and the woman, and between your offspring and hers; he will crush your head, and you will strike his heel" (Gen 3:15).

Because of their rebellion against God, conflict arises between humans. One of the important messages of Genesis 1–3 is that violence between humans is the result of human sin, not the result of the way God made us.

But, though he punishes his human creatures, God does not give up on them. Indeed, he pursues reconciliation with them. As the book of Genesis continues, the narrator describes humanity as dividing into those who rebel against God (Cain, those in the genealogy of Cain, the violent generation destroyed at the flood, the tower builders) and those who follow God (Abel, those in the genealogy of Seth, Noah, Abraham, and so on).

Right from the start we see God taking the side of the latter and punishing the former. While today, particularly among those in the Western church, the violence that God brings against his people's enemies is controversial.[3] The Old Testament gives us story after story of God's fighting against those who resist him and threaten his people. We only need to think of the flood, the plagues, and the drowning of Egyptian troops at the Re(e)d Sea, the conquest, and on and on. Throughout the history of Israel during Old Testament times, we can find stories where God fights the flesh-and-blood enemies of his people Israel.

But these are not the only stories we read in the Old Testament. We also hear about times when God brings the fight against his people.

PHASE TWO: GOD FIGHTS ISRAEL

Though our discussion of phase one may lead one to think, at least at first sight, God was not on Israel's side "right or wrong." When before the battle of Jericho, Joshua asked the commander of the army of the Lord (God himself): "Are you for us or for our enemies?" God answered, "Neither!" (Josh 5:13-14). Joshua learned this lesson in the next battle against Ai (Josh 7) when Israel failed to take that city due to the disobedience of one of its members. Or later during the period of the Judges during the time when Eli was judge and his two evil sons led the army: at that time, Israel lost not only the battle but also the ark of the covenant to the Philistines (1 Sam 4). Or in what is perhaps the most dramatic illustration of phase two, when God allowed and even assisted the Babylonians at the time they defeated unrepentant Judah, destroyed the temple, and deported its leading citizens. In response, the poet of Lamentations 2 knew that ultimately it was not Babylon but God himself who had come against Jerusalem "like an enemy" (Lam 2:4-5).

After all, they had been warned in the covenant that God had made with them at the time of Moses. God had told them that if they were obedient, then they would have victory over their enemies (Deut 28:7), but if they are disobedient, then "the LORD will cause you to be defeated before your enemies" (Deut 28:25). Israel, though God's chosen servant to mediate his blessing into the world, receives no favoritism when they resist him. Still he does not give up on them, as we learn as we now turn to phase three.

PHASE THREE: GOD WILL COME AND FIGHT FOR ISRAEL AGAINST THEIR OPPRESSORS

The Old Testament story does not end with Israel's leaders in exile. As we reviewed in our historical survey (see chap. 2), Persia defeated Babylon in 539 BC, and at that time its king, Cyrus, issued a decree that allowed Babylon's vassal nations, including Judah (2 Chron 36:23; Ezra 1:2-4) to return to their homelands and rebuild their temples. The books of Ezra and Nehemiah tell the story of some of those who returned in both the early postexilic period (539–515 BC) under the leadership of Sheshbazzar and Zerubbabel (Ezra 1–6) as well as later in the mid-fifth century under the leadership of Ezra and Nehemiah. The book of Esther, set in the first part of the fifth century, tells the story of Esther and Mordecai and others who choose not to return to the land at this time (the Diaspora).

Daniel lived into the early postexilic period but probably not too long into it since he must have been very old by this time and we have no account of him returning to the Promised Land. He also knew that, though the Persians allowed them to return to the land, in an important sense the exile was not done (see comments on the seventy "sevens" in Daniel 9 in chap. 12). God's people still lived under the oppression of their enemies. Daniel even saw into the future beyond his lifetime that one oppressor would follow another all the way to the end of time.

But he also saw, as we noted, that God the warrior would return in the future in order to judge their enemies and rescue his faithful ones. We have reviewed this message above when we looked particularly at

Daniel 7 in chapter ten; here I want to point out that Daniel is not alone with this message among the prophets of the postexilic period. These postexilic prophets carry the message of what I am calling phase three: that God will come and fight against their oppressors in the future.

For instance, Zechariah, who prophesied in the period soon after the Cyrus decree, concludes his book with a dramatic vision of the future "day of the LORD" (Zech 14:1). That day would see God come and destroy those who prey on his people. After the nations of the world gather against Jerusalem and capture it, "Then the LORD will go out and fight against those nations, as he fights on a day of battle" (Zech 14:3). God, of course, will be victorious on that day, and "the LORD will be king over the whole earth" (Zech 14:9).

Malachi, too, speaks of that future day of God's ultimate victory over those who resist him and oppress his people. He will also rescue his people.

> "Surely the day is coming; it will burn like a furnace. All the arrogant and every evildoer will be stubble, and the day that is coming will set them on fire," says the LORD Almighty. "Not a root or a branch will be left to them. But for you who revere my name, the sun of righteousness will rise with healing in its rays. And you will go out and frolic like well-fed calves. Then you will trample on the wicked; they will be ashes under the soles of your feet on the day when I act," says the LORD Almighty. (Mal 4:1-3)

The Old Testament, accordingly, ends with anticipation, the expectation that God will come as a warrior in the future to save them from their oppressors. Daniel, we have seen, contributes to this message, which rings out with the sure hope of God's rescue. Where does this expectation lead? We turn now to phase four and then phase five, which bring our attention to the message of the New Testament.

PHASE FOUR: JESUS FIGHTS THE SPIRITUAL POWERS AND AUTHORITIES

When we open the New Testament, we see that John the Baptist's message resonates with the same hope of judgment on those who stand against God, including those within the Jewish community whom he calls a "brood of vipers" (Mt 3:7). He warns these sinners to repent because the one coming after him "will baptize you with the Holy Spirit and fire. His winnowing fork is in his hand, and he will clear his threshing floor, gathering his wheat into the barn and burning up the chaff with unquenchable fire" (Mt 3:11-12).

When Jesus comes out to the wilderness, John recognizes him as the one he was expecting and baptizes him. Soon John is thrown in jail, and Jesus begins his earthly ministry. While in jail, John receives what to him are disturbing reports. Jesus is healing the sick, raising the dead, and preaching the good news to the poor. John responds by sending two of his disciples to Jesus with the question: "Are you the one who is to come, or should we expect someone else?" (Mt 11:3). We can hear John thinking to himself, *Where is the chaff burning?* Jesus, as it turns out, is not the Messiah John expected him to be.

For his part, Jesus tells these two men to go back and inform John about what they have seen—namely, that "the blind receive sight, the lame walk, those who have leprosy are cleansed, the deaf hear, the dead are raised, and the good news is proclaimed to the poor" (Mt 11:5). Through his actions then and in the future, Jesus is, in my own words, telling John, "Yes, I am the expected divine warrior. I have come to wage war against evil, but I have heightened and intensified the battle so that it is directed not toward evil humans but toward the spiritual powers and authorities. And these enemies are not defeated with weapons like spears and swords. Indeed, these enemies are not defeated by killing but by dying."

Thus, Jesus defeats the spiritual powers and authorities by going to the cross. Remember, when Jesus was arrested, Peter intervened and cut off the ear of the servant of the high priest who was part of the gang sent out to arrest him. Jesus rebuked Peter by saying, "Put your sword back in its place. . . . Do you think I cannot call on my Father, and he will at once put at my disposal more than twelve legions of angels? But how then would the Scriptures be fulfilled that say it must happen in this way?" (Mt 26:52-54).

Jesus defeated the powers and authorities on the cross, which is why Paul uses military language to describe the crucifixion ("And having disarmed the powers and authorities, he made a public spectacle of them, triumphing over them by the cross," Col 2:15) and the ascension ("This is why it says: 'When he ascended on high, he took many captives and gave gifts to his people,'" Eph 4:8).

But was John the Baptist wrong in his expectation? Or for that matter, was Daniel wrong? After all, after Jesus died, was raised, and ascended in power, evil human kingdoms continued to oppress the followers of God. The kingdom of God has come, but not fully. As we turn to phase five, we come to understand what John the Baptist and certainly Daniel did not understand about the significance of their message. Jesus, the messianic divine warrior, was not going to come just once, but twice.

PHASE FIVE: JESUS DEFEATS ALL EVIL ONCE AND FOR ALL

We learn about phase five from those passages that talk about Jesus' return at the end of history. Jesus' defeat of the spiritual powers and authorities on the cross assures victory at the end, but in the meantime evil still exists in the world. The people of God still live in an evil world with cultures of various levels of toxicity to their faith, but the time will come when, in the words of Daniel, "The God of heaven will set up a kingdom that will never be destroyed, nor will it be left to another people. It will crush all those kingdoms and bring them to an end, but it will itself endure forever. This is the meaning of the vision of the rock cut out of a mountain, but not by human hands" (Dan 2:44-45).

DANIEL IN THE LITTLE APOCALYPSE OF THE GOSPEL (MARK 13 AND SYNOPTIC PARALLELS)

Jesus himself informed his disciples of his future return, citing a number of Old Testament passages, but for our purposes we are particularly drawn to his use of key passages from the book of Daniel. On a visit to the temple, the disciples express their amazement at the grandeur of the temple: "Look, Teacher! What massive stones! What magnificent buildings" (Mk 13:1). Jesus for his part tells them that the day is coming when the temple will be destroyed. The disciples then question Jesus, "Tell us, when will these things happen? And what will be the sign that they are all about to be fulfilled?" (Mk 13:4).

In response, Jesus speaks of future social and even cosmic turmoil. He warns his followers that they must preach the gospel to all the nations and in the process they will be arrested and put on trial. He warns them that "everyone will hate you because of me, but the one who stands firm to the end will be saved" (Mk 13:13).

Then he gives the first reference to Daniel: "When you see 'the abomination that causes desolation' standing where it does not belong—let the reader understand—then let those who are in Judea flee to the mountains" (Mk 13:14, referring to Dan 9:27; 11:31; 12:11). In the book of Daniel, it is likely that the reference was to Antiochus Epiphanes, who set up a meteorite sacred to Zeus in the temple in Jerusalem, so this reference in Mark has typically been understood to refer to some kind of analogous despoiling of something holy, but exactly what that will be is left unspecified.

The second reference to Daniel comes when Jesus speaks of the intervention that will take place in the midst of the chaos: "At that time people will see the Son of Man coming in clouds with great power and glory. And he will send his angels and gather his elect from the four winds, from the ends of the earth to the ends of the heavens" (Mk 13:26-27). The allusion to Daniel 7:13-14 is clear, where the one like a son of man riding the cloud (the divine war chariot) goes to battle against the forces of evil represented by the four beasts that arise out of the sea and ultimately the boastful horn. In this way, Jesus tells his disciples that the expectation of Daniel will come to its full conclusion with his second return that is described here and elsewhere (besides the parallel accounts of this speech [Mt 24:30; Lk 21:27], see also Rev 1:7). Jesus ends this speech by telling his disciples that no one will know the time that he will return and so they need to be perpetually ready (Mk 13:32-37). Indeed, the signs that he gives the disciples (wars, social unrest, claims of false messiahs, earthquakes, famines) happen all the time and are simply reminders that the end has not come, not special indications that we are getting close to the end. What Jesus says at the end of this speech is a strong reminder that it is a misuse of Daniel or any other biblical text to try to determine when Jesus will return.

DANIEL IN REVELATION

The little apocalypse in the Gospels anticipates the fuller description of Jesus' return in the book of Revelation. Here we will begin with a look at the specific connection between Daniel and Revelation before showing the conceptual connection between the message of Daniel and the book of Revelation.

The book opens by describing itself as a "revelation from Jesus Christ." The Greek word for "revelation" is *apocalypsis* from which we get our English term "apocalypse" and the adjective "apocalyptic." From this Greek word, scholars derive the term "apocalypse" to describe other texts that share the genre with Revelation, and Daniel is, as we saw in chapter one, an example, perhaps the best or even only example of the genre in the Old Testament.

In our earlier study, we noted a feature of apocalyptic literature to be its distinctive mode of God's communication. In the Old Testament book, God never spoke directly to Daniel but rather sent his angel (on occasion identified as Gabriel) to interpret his vision. In the book of Revelation, John receives a revelation, and Jesus sends him an un-named angel to make it known to him (Rev 1:2). However, rather than keeping his revelation to himself as Daniel did, John writes a letter to the seven churches of Asia and after conferring a blessing on the recipients (Rev 1:4-6), he suddenly exclaims: "'Look, he is coming with the clouds,' and 'every eye will see him, even those who pierced him'; and all peoples on earth 'will mourn because of him.' So shall it be! Amen" (Rev 1:7). As in the little apocalypses, Jesus' return is pictured as him riding the storm cloud into battle. As we will see, this battle culminates in God's fight against the evil powers as well as evil human beings anticipated by Daniel and John the Baptist.

But before getting there, we should also notice the similarities and differences in the interaction between God and his servant in the final vision of Daniel and the book of Revelation. In the former, Daniel reports that he "looked up and there before me was a man dressed in linen, with a belt of fine gold from Uphaz around his waist. His body was like topaz, his face like lightning, his eyes like flaming torches, his arms and legs like the gleam of burnished bronze, and his voice like the sound of a multitude" (Dan 10:5-6). In Revelation, John states that he turned around at the sound of a voice,

> and among the lampstands was someone like a son of man, dressed in a robe reaching down to his feet and with a golden sash around his chest. The hair on his head was white like wool, as white as snow, and his eyes were like blazing fire. His feet were like bronze glowing in a furnace, and his voice was like the sound of rushing waters. In his right hand he held seven stars, and coming out of his mouth was a sharp, double-edged sword. His face was like the sun shining in all its brilliance. (Rev 1:13-16)

Both figures are described with similes that highlight their majestic splendor. Sometimes the similes overlap. The figure in Daniel has a belt of fine gold, a face like lightning, eyes like flaming torches, arms and legs like burnished bronze, and a voice that resonated with the sound of a multitude. The figure in Revelation has a golden sash, a face like the sun, eyes like blazing fire, feet like bronze, and a voice like the sound of rushing waters. Similar, we see, though not quite identical features.

The main differences in this depiction begin with the identity of the figure. In the Old Testament, the glorious figure is God himself, while in Revelation it is the risen and ascended Christ. Indeed, we should take special note that Revelation refers to him as "like a son of man," yet another reference to Daniel 7:13-14.

Thus, the introduction to the book of Revelation prepares us for a Daniel-like prophecy of the future. Not that there are a lot of specific quotations to the book of Daniel, but there are allusions and similarities because John relates his vision of a future intervention of the divine warrior to judge the evil spiritual and human powers that threaten and harass God's people.

To the church of Philadelphia, Jesus proclaims, "I am coming soon" (Rev 3:11). While Gabriel tells Daniel to "roll up and seal the words of the scroll until the time of the end" (Dan 12:4), John describes how Jesus is the one "worthy to take the scroll and to open its seals" (Rev 5:9). In a setting reminiscent of the judgment rendered the Ancient of Days, who was surrounded by "thousands upon thousands," then "ten thousand times ten thousand" angels who "stood before him" (Dan 7:10), so before rendering judgment, John hears "the voice of many angels, numbering thousands upon thousands, and ten thousand times ten thousand" (Rev 5:11). They encircle the throne (on which Jesus is sitting) and praise him: "Worthy is the Lamb, who was slain, to receive power and wealth and wisdom and strength and honor and glory and praise!" (Rev 5:12). As he opens what turns out to be seven seals, judgments are unleashed on the earth (Rev 6:1–8:5).

Evil itself is pictured as a seven-headed beast with ten horns and seven heads coming out of the sea (Rev 13). This beast is reminiscent of the monsters that rise out of the sea in Daniel 7. The ten horns remind us of the fourth beast in Daniel with its ten horns. But other Old Testament texts also reverberate here, in particular the language of the many-headed Leviathan (Ps 74:12-15; Is 27:1). While the number of heads is not mentioned in the Old Testament, ancient Ugaritic texts in the Baal cycle mention a seven-headed sea monster Lotan (the Ugaritic equivalent to the biblical Leviathan) who represents the forces of chaos that the creator god must subdue to bring order. Over against this and other beasts representing spiritual and human evil, is one who is "seated on a cloud"—namely, "one like a son of man with a crown of gold on his head and a sharp sickle in his hand" (Rev 14:14) to whom an angel calls, "Take your sickle and reap, because the time to reap has come, for the harvest of the earth is ripe" (Rev 14:15). In this work, Jesus is joined by two other angels, who reap the earth and throw the gathered grapes into "the great winepress of God's wrath. They were trampled in the winepress outside the city, and blood flowed out of the press, rising as high as the horses' bridles for a distance of 1,600 stadia" (Rev 14:19-20).

Similar beast imagery is found in Revelation 17. In this chapter, a woman representing Babylon (standing for contemporary Rome and beyond to all future evil oppressive human empires) rides a beast again described as having seven heads and ten horns (Rev 17:3). This woman and her beasts are seen as emanating from the waters (Rev 17:15). She was "drunk with the blood of God's holy people, the blood of those who bore testimony to Jesus" (Rev 17:6). This woman and her beast and the heads and horns that represent kings "will wage war against the Lamb, but the Lamb will triumph over them because he is the Lord of lords and King of kings—and with him will be his called, chosen and faithful followers" (Rev 17:14).

The future victory over the beast and those who follow it is described in the magnificent and powerful scene described in Revelation 19:11-21. Here, in a passage filled with allusions and miniquotations from Deuteronomy, Psalms, and Isaiah that describe Yahweh the warrior, Jesus rides out at the head of an army to wage war and render judgment. The end of the chapter describes the final battle that once and for all brings evil to an end:

> Then I saw the beast and the kings of the earth and their armies gathered together to wage war against the rider on the horse and his army. But the beast was captured, and with it the false prophet who had performed the signs on its behalf. With these signs he had deluded those who had received the mark of the beast and worshiped its image. The two of them were thrown alive into the fiery lake of burning sulfur. The rest were killed with the sword coming out of the mouth of the rider on the horse, and all the birds gorged themselves on their flesh. (Rev 19:19-21)

In this passage we see the ultimate and full accomplishment of that which Daniel's visions anticipated. In spite of present trouble, God is indeed in control, and he will have the final victory. God judges evil and saves his people. He establishes his eternal kingdom, here described in the Bible's culminating vision of the new Jerusalem in which "there was no longer any sea" (or monsters of the sea; Rev 21:1), for all threat and danger has been quelled.

IMPLICATIONS FOR OUR LIVES TODAY

Thus, we see how the message of Daniel fits into the biblical theology of God's warfare against evil. Its message is that God will come in the future and defeat our enemies (phase three) and anticipates the twofold coming of Jesus (phases four and five). Now that we can see where Daniel fits into the biblical message, we can ask the important question: What does the book of Daniel say to us today in regard to where we are in God's developing war against evil? Daniel lived in a toxic culture but with hope that his God would return to save his people and judge their enemies. The New Testament proclaims that God has come in the person of Christ and has defeated evil on the cross. But it also tells us that his victory, while assuring the final outcome, is still to be fully realized in the future. We live in what we have called phase four, the time after the cross but before the return of Christ. Thus, we too live in hope of Christ's return while we still live in a toxic world ("Amen. Come, Lord Jesus," Rev 22:20).

But how do we live in the light of these biblical teachings?

LIVING CONFIDENTLY IN A TROUBLED WORLD

In chapter fifteen, we explored the significance of the six stories about Daniel for our lives today. There we observed that, like Daniel and his three friends, we too live in cultures that are toxic to our faith. In some cultures today (China, Iran, and North Korea, to name only a few), the hostility of the broader culture is obvious. While the toxicity of the culture may be more subtle in the United States, Europe, Australia, New Zealand, and South Korea (to name a few), we delude ourselves if we think that the culture is or ever will be friendly to Christianity. Indeed, if we feel that the culture is friendly, we are likely compromising ourselves to it either by integrating our faith to the culture (the sin of the so-called religious left) or by trying to co-opt the power of the state to coerce others to act like Christians (the sin of the so-called religious right). While there is nothing wrong with trying to persuade the broader culture toward Christian values, there is everything wrong with trying to use the power of the state to make non-Christians act like Christians. In my opinion there is nothing wrong, indeed it is admirable, for Christians to become politicians and then to work toward moving our society through persuasion toward biblical values. But the temptation will be strong on those who do achieve political power to use typical strong-arm tactics and to adopt voter-pleasing (and perhaps more to the point donor-pleasing) policies rather than thinking through the issues based on biblical principles. Politicians of that type deserve no respect, especially if they are Christians.

Living in the tension of our faith and the values of our broader culture can lead to great anxiety in our lives as we navigate where we need to withdraw, publicly protest, try to transform our society, or simply live in our own daily and professional lives. By looking at Daniel 1–6, we saw that there is not a one-size-fits-all approach to culture. Daniel himself adopted different strategies as he lived within his society.

Daniel 7–12 gave Daniel's original readers the long view to help them live with confidence in a troubled world. His message resonated and resonates with the generations that follow him down to the present day. In the light of the future, Daniel comforts us with the message that in spite of present circumstances (we live in a toxic culture), God will have the final victory.

Because of this, we can live with confidence even in a troubled world. Today anxieties arise from many sectors over which we personally have no control. For many the economic collapse of 2008 brought financial trouble and reminds us that no matter how good the economy is, it can collapse again through market forces beyond our control. 9/11 and other comparable terrorist acts throughout the world demonstrate the fragility of life. But threat comes into our lives in a variety of more personal ways as well. Just this morning on the news came the report of the murder of a jogger on the streets of a relatively crime-free neighborhood in Washington, DC. The woman was jogging on a well-traveled street in the early evening, and as she passed a person, he stabbed her fatally in the neck. She died on the way to the hospital. These stories remind us that life can be suddenly snatched away. But death is not our only anxiety. Another serious problem today is drug addiction. Our lives can be suddenly turned around by an addiction problem of ourselves or a loved one.

Simply put, life can be overwhelming, and we can be engulfed by our anxieties. But Christians can live without fear in spite of our suffering or the uncertainties of the future. Why? Because we know the end of the story. Daniel tells us that God will intervene at the end of history to bring judgment on evil and to rescue his people. Daniel also informs us that even if we faithfully suffer to the time of our deaths, we will eventually "awake . . . to everlasting life" (Dan 12:2). The New Testament, as we have seen, takes Daniel's hope and gives us even further insight into it as it describes the two comings of Jesus.

Indeed, this knowledge should lead to the "perfect love [of God that] drives out fear" (1 Jn 4:18) and the "peace of God, which transcends all understanding" (Phil 4:7). Christians, who are confident in the end of the story, which is our story, can be risk takers. We do not have to cower in fear of the next terrorist attack or of a random shooting or the influx of illegal immigrants into our country because we know the ultimate outcome of the future—God's victory. Unfortunately, Christians today are not known for this type of courage, but just the opposite.

We must remember that our hope is not based on knowledge of when Jesus will come back (remember that it is not the purpose of Daniel or any biblical book to give us that kind of information). He could come back tomorrow or the next day or in five years or thousands of years from now. We don't know, and it doesn't really matter in the light of eternity.

Notice the final words that the interpreting angel speaks to Daniel. They are not "withdraw from the world and prepare for the end," they are "go your way till the end. You will rest, and then at the end of the days you will rise to receive your allotted inheritance" (Dan 12:13). These are good words for Daniel and for us: live your life until you die knowing that you will rise again.

This life will not be easy. It is a battle. As we turn to the next section, we will see that God calls us to engage in the battle of life with confidence in spite of the fact that our enemies are none other than the spiritual powers and authorities.

ENGAGE IN THE SPIRITUAL BATTLE

Daniel 7–12 speaks of God's future intervention in a troubled world where he rescues his people and judges their oppressors (phase three). This message comes at the end of the Old Testament period during which God had fought evil in the form of Israel's enemies (phase one) and, on occasion, Israel itself (phase two). Above, we observed that the New Testament reveals that God's future intervention would come in two phases. Today, phase four (Jesus fights the spiritual powers and authorities) is in our past; phase five (Jesus wins the final battle against spiritual and human enemies) is in our future. How should we live in phase four?

First, while embracing our place in God's battle against evil, we should not disown God's battles during the Old Testament time period. As we will see, our battle takes a different shape, but that should not lead us to demean God's work in the past. Jesus himself fully affirmed the Old Testament story, including its accounts of God bringing violent judgment against people who resisted him; we should as well.

But we do indeed live in a time of spiritual warfare, not physical warfare. Those of us who live in the period between the first and second coming of Christ must never use physical force in the furtherance of the church's agenda or in the name of Christ. Paul could not be clearer on this subject:

> Finally, be strong in the Lord and in his mighty power. Put on the full armor of God, so that you can take your stand against the devil's schemes. For our struggle is not against flesh and blood, but against the rulers, against the authorities, against the powers

of this dark world and against the spiritual forces of evil in the heavenly realms. (Eph 6:10-12)

Our battle is against spiritual, not human, evil. We should note that the spiritual battle has been ongoing since even before the creation of human beings as implied by the appearance of the serpent in the garden (Gen 3:1), a force ultimately identified as the devil (Rom 16:20; Rev 12:3), a power that worked at odds with God's good purpose in creation. We only get glimpses of the battle between God and his angels and the spiritual forces of evil. The latter likely stand behind at least some of the appearances of Leviathan (especially Is 27:1), but the clearest glimpse comes in Daniel 10 when Gabriel describes the fight between Michael and the spirit princes of Persia and Greece.

Still, while we do get the occasional allusion to a spiritual battle in the Old Testament, it is not until after the resurrection that we are invited into the battle. Paul goes on here and in 2 Corinthians to tell Christians that such a battle is not won with the use of physical weapons but rather spiritual ones. In Ephesians 6, after stating that our battle is against the spiritual powers, he continues:

Therefore put on the full armor of God, so that when the day of evil comes, you may be able to stand your ground, and after you have done everything, to stand. Stand firm then, with the belt of truth buckled around your waist, with the breastplate of righteousness in place, and with your feet fitted with the readiness that comes from the gospel of peace. In addition to all this, take up the shield of faith, with which you can extinguish all the flaming arrows of the evil one. Take the helmet of salvation and the sword of the Spirit, which is the word of God. And pray in the Spirit on all occasions with all kinds of prayers and requests. (Eph 6:13-18)

And in 2 Corinthians, he informs his readers:

For though we live in the world, we do not wage war as the world does. The weapons we fight with are not the weapons of the world. On the contrary, they have divine power to demolish strongholds. We demolish arguments and every pretension that sets itself up against the knowledge of God, and we take captive every thought to make it obedient to Christ. And we will be ready to punish every act of disobedience, once your obedience is complete. (2 Cor 10:3-6)

FIGHTING EVIL IN THE WORLD

No matter where we live today, we encounter the forces of evil in the world. We read about injustice and corruption in every sector of society. The powers and principalities present their threat through the evil actions of human beings as they prey on others and take advantage of them sexually, psychologically, financially, and/or relationally. We can find such evil in family life, politics, business, the military, the church, and so on.

Evangelical Christians often agree on the nature of evil in the world. At the moment of writing, sexual abuse is in the forefront of the news thanks to the #metoo movement. There is no defense for taking advantage of another person's body against her or his will for sexual pleasure, whether that happens in a family, Hollywood, government, and most especially the church. Christians who engage in the spiritual battle fight against the harm of sexual abuse using all the spiritual tools at our disposal.

Other issues like racism and pervasive poverty are also evils that must be resisted. Christians may disagree how these issues should be addressed, but to see humans created in the image of God struggle by being demeaned is unacceptable.

In a recent, incisive article, the Reverend Eugene F. Rivers notes that Martin Luther King Jr.'s "political movement . . . was a movement of the Holy Spirit." King recognized that "white supremacism, economic oppression, and militarism—are spiritual realities in their own right, demonic powers that must be combatted with spiritual weapons." Rivers also worries about the present reactions to the white supremacist movement, including some, but not all, aspects of the Black Lives

Matter movement and more clearly Antifa, "that are easily sucked into the spirit of the demons themselves as they resort to violence, anger, and hate." Rivers urges that Christian activists recognize that this is a spiritual battle that needs to use spiritual weapons, not guns or clubs or knives, to fight the systemic evil that lies behind racism.[4] Yes, the evil of white supremacy needs to be called out for the evil that it is and resisted, but to use street violence against them brings the resistance down to their low level. There is absolutely nothing wrong with righteous anger, but righteous anger cannot be expressed on the streets with knives, clubs, or other weapons.

We could go on with other injustices where Christians agree that evil is raising its ugly head, but there are also a number of issues on which Christians would disagree. Is all war evil, or is there such a thing as a just war? Is capital punishment an appropriate penalty for murder, or should it be eradicated as part of a consistent ethic of life? While most would agree that exploiting the environment is wrong, there would be disagreement over where such harm is happening today and what should be done about it. Witness, for instance, the debate over climate change.

This book is not the place to adjudicate these debated issues.[5] What we can all agree on is that there is plenty of evil in our lives and our society that God calls on us to engage in the spiritual battle, which can take many forms depending on the situation. It may be prayer, mobilizing people to a righteous cause, supporting a candidate that we believe would bring more justice in our society, and on and on. We can't fight on every front, but God calls us to bring our faith prayerfully and in the power of the Spirit to resist the onslaught of evil in the world.

EXTENDING THE KINGDOM OF LIGHT
AGAINST THE KINGDOM OF DARKNESS

Fighting evil "out there" does not simply mean protesting and working against the various human and spiritual forms of evil that we have talked about in the previous section. While in the Old Testament period God's people were to be a holy people that kept separate from the ungodly with the hope that they would, like a Ruth, come and join them in worship of God, in the New Testament, Jesus' followers were to go out to the nations: "Therefore go and make disciples of all the nations, baptizing them in the name of the Father and of the Son and of the Holy Spirit, and teaching them to obey everything I have commanded you. And surely I am with you always, to the very end of the age" (Mt 28:19-20).

God's people are thus to go out to share the gospel with the hope that others will believe and will be baptized and join the growing ranks of the church. In this light, it is interesting to hear Paul in the letter to the Colossians describe baptism as a form of death:

> For in Christ all the fullness of the Deity lives in bodily form, and in Christ you have been brought to fullness. He is the head over every power and authority. In him you were also circumcised with a circumcision not performed by human hands. Your whole self ruled by the flesh was put off when you were circumcised by Christ, having been buried with him in baptism, in which you were also raised with him through your faith in the working of God, who raised him from the dead. (Col 2:9-12)

When someone hears and gospel and accepts it, the old person dies, and the new person rises up. As we share the gospel we offer the opportunity for people to leave the kingdom of darkness and join the kingdom of light. Through evangelism, God strikes a blow against the spiritual powers and authorities.

FIGHTING EVIL IN OUR OWN HEARTS

Yes, there is evil out there that must be challenged, but we must always do so being aware of the evil that remains in our own hearts. Once someone becomes a new person, they don't immediately become perfect. Sin remains in our hearts and will remain until we die. The difference is that we wage war against the darkness of our hearts. While some think Paul in Romans 7:14-24 is talking about himself preconversion, it seems to me that he is describing the battle that goes on in every Christian's heart:

We know that the law is spiritual; but I am unspiritual, sold as a slave to sin. I do not understand what I do. For what I want to do I do not do, but what I hate I do. And if I do what I do not want to do, I agree that the law is good. As it is, it is no longer I myself who do it, but it is sin living in me. For I know that good itself does not dwell in me, that is, in my sinful nature. For I have the desire to do what is good, but I cannot carry it out. For I do not do the good I want to do, but the evil I do not want to do—this I keep on doing. Now if I do what I do not want to do, it is no longer I who do it, but it is sin living in me that does it.

So I find this law at work: Although I want to do good, evil is right there with me. For in my inner being I delight in God's law; but I see another law at work in me, waging war against the law of my mind and making me a prisoner of the law of sin at work within me. What a wretched man I am! Who will rescue me from this body that is subject to death?

Paul delights in God's law in his inner being, but the law of his mind brings him back to sin and subjects him to the law of sin. These two laws, he says, are "waging war" within him. It sounds hopeless, but it is not. Why? Because Jesus wages war against the evil of his mind. He cannot save himself, but Jesus can. For this reason, Paul ends with doxology not lament:

Thanks be to God, who delivers me through Jesus Christ our Lord!

CONCLUSION

Daniel 7–12 gives us four visions that emphasize the major theme of Daniel in what we might call a cosmic sense. In spite of present troubles, God is in control, and he will have the final victory. Like Daniel's original audience, we live in a time of trouble, whether we reside in the relatively tolerant West or in a country where Christians experience active persecution. We too, therefore, need to hear about God's control and ultimate victory. The fundamental truth of these visions is that God will rescue his people and judge those who hate him.

Looking at the message of Daniel 7–12 in the context of the whole canon allowed us to see where its message fits in God's fight against evil. In particular we remarked that Daniel's message anticipates the coming of Jesus the warrior. The New Testament makes it clear that he is the "one like a son of man" (Dan 7:13-14) who will bring an end to all spiritual and human evil.

DISCUSSION QUESTIONS

1. Describe in your own words the five phases of God's war against evil as described in this chapter.

2. Where does the church fit into this warfare today?

3. How do we engage in spiritual warfare?

4. When you think of Christ's return how does that make you feel? Why?

Appendix

Commentaries on the Book of Daniel

For further study and for future reference, I recommend the following commentaries.

Goldingay, J. *Daniel*. Word, 1989. liii/351 pages.

Goldingay's is perhaps the most comprehensive commentary on Daniel listed here. He gives insight into historical, literary, and theological issues concerning the book. He also demonstrates an amazing grasp of the secondary literature. As opposed to the position taken in this present book, Goldingay argues that Daniel was written in the second century BC.

House, P. R. *Daniel*. TOTC. InterVarsity, 2018. 208 pages.

A helpful, very recent overview of the book of Daniel geared for pastors and interested laypeople.

Longman, Tremper, III. *Daniel*. NIVAC. Zondervan, 1999. 313 pages.

In keeping with the design of the NIVAC series, I explore the original meaning and contemporary significance of this interesting yet often enigmatic biblical book. In addition, I explain how I move from the ancient text to our modern situation. Daniel becomes, in the first six chapters, a study of how a person of faith not only copes but thrives in a hostile cultural setting. In the last half of the book, it raises the question of how we are to understand the apocalyptic sections of Scripture that describe the end of history. The theme of the whole book is, in spite of present difficult circumstances, God is in control and will defeat the forces of evil and oppression.

Lucas, E. C. *Daniel*. AOTC. InterVarsity, 2002. 359 pages.
Lucas is sensitive to Daniel as literature and theology. He provides a special study of the ancient Near Eastern background to the imagery in chapters seven to twelve. Many, however, including myself, will find his arguments in favor of a second-century date for the book not persuasive, though he does argue in a way that is consistent with a high view of biblical authority.

Miller, S. M. *Daniel*. NAC. Broadman, 1994. 348 pages.
Miller writes competently in defense of a conservative approach to the book. He concentrates on historical issues and the basic theological message. In the apocalyptic sections, he adopts a literal (plain) reading of the text.

Widder, W. L. *Daniel*. SOG. Grand Rapids: Zondervan, 2016. 288 pages.
Widder gives an excellent interpretation of the book of Daniel in its original context as well as a robust discussion of how the book anticipates Christ and has significance for our lives today.

Young, E. J. *The Prophecy of Daniel*. Banner of Truth, 1949. 330 pages.
The importance of this commentary is found in its firm and intelligent conservative stance. Young polemicizes against critical and dispensationalist approaches. He is not particularly sensitive to the literary nature or biblical theology of the book, but he is an excellent language scholar.

Notes

1 STORIES AND VISIONS IN THE MIDST OF OPPRESSION: GENRE, LANGUAGE, AND STRUCTURE

[1]Hans Frei, *The Eclipse of Biblical Narrative* (New Haven: Yale University Press, 1974).

[2]The following is indebted to the landmark studies by W. L. Humphreys, "A Lifestyle for Diaspora: A Study of the Tales of Esther and Daniel," *Journal of Biblical Literature* 92 (1973): 211-23, and L. M. Wills, *The Jew in the Court of the Foreign King* (Minneapolis: Fortress Press, 1990).

[3]For some unexplained reason the NIV relegates the phrase "in Aramaic" to a footnote.

2 BABYLONIAN EXILE AND PERSIAN (AND GREEK) DOMINATION: THE HISTORICAL SETTING OF THE BOOK OF DANIEL

[1]Genesis 1–2 asserts that God created everything and everyone but does not claim to tell us how God did it by presenting these broad historical truths using figurative language. See T. Longman III, *Confronting Old Testament Controversies: Pressing Questions About Evolution, Sexuality, History, and Violence* (Grand Rapids: Baker Books, 2019).

[2]In later Old Testament history, when the people of God grew beyond an extended family, the altar was incorporated into the tabernacle and ultimately the temple. See T. Longman III, *Immanuel in Our Place: Seeing Christ in Israel's Worship* (Phillipsburg, NJ: P&R, 2001).

[3]For more detail on Genesis 3–11, see T. Longman III, *How to Read Genesis* (Downers Grove, IL: InterVarsity Press, 2009), 101-25.

[4]T. Longman III, *The Story of God Bible Commentary: Genesis* (Grand Rapids: Zondervan, 2016), 159-61.

[5]Highlighted in the study by Joel S. Kaminsky, *Yet I Loved Jacob: Reclaiming the Biblical Concept of Election* (Nashville: Abingdon, 2007).

[6]For more detail on this period, see T. Longman III, *How to Read Exodus* (Downers Grove, IL: InterVarsity Press, 2009).

[7]P. Borgman, *David, Saul, and God: Rediscovering an Ancient Story* (New York: Oxford University Press, 2008).

[8]In the NIV (and other translations) of Daniel 5:2, Nebuchadnezzar seems to be identified as Belshazzar's father. A better translation of the Hebrew word in this context would be either ancestor or predecessor (as in the NIV footnote).

[9]Translations of the Prayer of Nabonidus from Baruch A. Levine in vol. 1 of *The Context of Scripture*, ed. William W. Hallo (Leiden: Brill, 1997–2002), 286.

[10]P.-A. Beaulieu, "The Babylonian Background of the Fiery Furnace in Daniel 3," *Journal of Biblical Literature* 128 (2009): 275-76.

[11]H. H. Rowley, *Darius the Mede and the Four World Empires in the Book of Daniel* (Cardiff: University of Wales Press Board, 1935), 54.

[12]A theory put forward by J. C. Whitcomb, *Darius the Mede: A Study in Historical Identification* (Grand Rapids: Eerdmans, 1959).

[13]D. J. Wiseman, *Chronicles of the Chaldean Kings* (London: British Museum Publications, Ltd., 1956).

[14]S. D. Anderson and R. C. Young, "The Remembrance of Daniel's Darius the Mede in Berossus and Harpocration," *Bibliotheca Sacra* 173 (2016): 315-23.

[15]One of the more intriguing hypotheses is that of W. H. Shea, "Darius the Mede: An Update," *Andrews University Seminary Studies* 20 (1982): 229-47. This article is a capstone of a series of articles on the subject published in the journal *Andrews University Seminary Studies* beginning in 1971. His viewpoint was critiqued by L. L. Grabbe, "Another Look at the Gestalt of 'Darius the Mede,'" *Catholic Biblical Quarterly* 50 (1988), 198-213.

[16]The Cyrus Cylinder, a Persian text contemporary with Cyrus, indicates that this decree was not special for the Jewish people, but extended to many of Babylon's former vassals. The Persian policy attempted to maintain control in the empire by granting certain limited freedoms to their vassal people.

[17]The non-Christian Neo-Platonic philosopher Porphyry of Tyre (AD 233–304) is often cited as a precursor to this view.

[18]For more on historical criticism and its antisupernatural bias, see T. Longman III, "History and Old Testament Interpretation," in *Hearing the Old Testament: Listening for God's Address,* ed. C. G. Bartholomew and D. J. H. Beldman (Grand Rapids: Eerdmans, 2012), 96-121.

[19]W. S. Towner, *Daniel,* Interpretation (Louisville: Westminster John Knox, 1984), 115.

[20]We can find this type of argument in John E. Goldingay, *Daniel,* WBC (Nashville: Thomas Nelson, 1989); E. Lucas, *Daniel,* Apollos (Downers Grove, IL: InterVarsity Press, 2002); W. B. Nelson, *Daniel,* UBCS (Grand Rapids: Baker, 2013).

[21]W. W. Hallo, "Akkadian Apocalypses," *Israel Exploration Journal* 16 (1966): 133-41.

[22]These Akkadian texts were the subject of my doctoral dissertation, which was published as *Fictional Akkadian Autobiography: A Generic and Comparative Study* (Winona Lake, IN: Eisenbrauns, 1991).

3 COMFORT IN THE MIDST OF OPPRESSION: THE THEME OF THE BOOK

[1]A number of recent studies have highlighted the presence of themes of resistance in the book of Daniel. See, for example, D. L. Smith-Christopher, "Prayers and Dreams: Power and Diaspora Identity in the Social Setting of the Daniel Tales," in J. J. Collins and P. W. Flint (eds.), *The Book of Daniel: Composition and Reception,* VTSup, 83.1 (Boston: Brill Academic, 2001), 1:266-90, and A. E. Portier-Young, *Apocalypse Against Empire: Theologies of Resistance in Early Judaism* (Grand Rapids: Eerdmans, 2011). For a well-balanced perspective recognizing both themes of resistance and accommodation, see C. A. Newsom, "Political Theology in the Book of Daniel: An Internal Debate," *Review and Expositor* 109: 557-68.

4 FORCED TO TRAIN IN A HOSTILE ENVIRONMENT, PART 1: DANIEL 1

[1]For examples of ancient Near Eastern treaties (both Neo-Assyrian as well as Hittite), see vol. 2 of *The Context of Scripture,* ed. William W. Hallo (Leiden: Brill, 1997–2002), 93-106, 327-32.

[2]See the Marduk Prophecy (Hallo, ed., *Context of Scripture* 1:480-81), which describes the movements of the Marduk statue and alludes to the

time that the Hittite king Murshilis defeated Babylon and took the cult statue in 1551 BC and when the Assyrian king Tukulti-Ninurta I defeated Kashtiliash IV and took the statue to Assyria.

[3]Jeremiah acknowledges this in Jer 3:16.

[4]Jin Hee Han, *Daniel's Spiel: Apocalyptic Literacy in the Book of Daniel* (Lanham, MD: University Press of America, 2008), 24.

[5]Examples of the Amarna Letters may be found in *Ancient Near Eastern Texts Relating to the Old Testament*, ed. James B. Pritchard (Princeton: Princeton University Press, 1969), 483-90.

[6]See T. Longman III and J. H. Walton, *The Lost World of the Flood: Mythology, Theology, and the Deluge Debate* (Downers Grove, IL: InterVarsity Press, 2018), 53-90.

[7]A. Leo Oppenheim, *The Interpretation of Dreams in the Ancient Near East with a Translation of an Assyrian Dream Book* (Transactions of the American Philosophical Society NS 46: Philadelphia: American Philosophical Society, 1956).

[8]A. Leo Oppenheim, *Ancient Mesopotamia: Portrait of a Dead Empire* (Chicago: Chicago University Press, 1977), 183-97.

5 FORCED TO TRAIN IN A HOSTILE ENVIRONMENT, PART 2: DANIEL 2

[1]Translation from Longman, *Proverbs*, BCOTWP (Grand Rapids: Baker, 2006).

[2]See Longman, *The Fear of the Lord Is Wisdom* (Grand Rapids: Baker Academic, 2017), for a sustained argument that "fear of the Lord" is the central thesis of Proverbs, Job, and Ecclesiastes.

[3]J. Calvin, *Daniel I (Chapters 1–6)* (Grand Rapids: Eerdmans, 1993), 76-77.

[4]A less likely reason for his insistence that someone tell him what he dreamed is that he could not remember it because it was disturbing.

7 WHO CAN INTERPRET THE WRITING ON THE WALL?: DANIEL 5

[1]The Nabonidus Chronicle, which is a part of the Babylonian Chronicles.

[2]K. Jobes, *Esther*, NIVAC (Grand Rapids: Zondervan, 1999).

[3]It is often pointed out that Nebuchadnezzar is here called Belshazzar's "father" (*'ab*) when we know that neither he nor his real father, Nabonidus,

was a blood descendant of Nebuchadnezzar. However, there is some evidence that the family was related by marriage, and in any case 'ab can mean "predecessor" rather than "father" or "ancestor" in this place.

[4]In a persuasive article, A. Wolters ("Untying the King's Knots: Physiology and Wordplay in Daniel 5," *Journal of Biblical Literature* 110 [1991], 117-22) examines the Aramaic of this verse and determines that the last clause is better understood as "wetting his pants."

[5]Thus providing support to the idea that Belshazzar was a coregent at this time.

[6]A. Wolters, "The Riddle of the Scales in Daniel 5," *Hebrew Union College Annual* 62 (1991):155-77.

[7]See pp. 27-28.

8 THE THREE FRIENDS AND THE FIERY FURNACE: DANIEL 3

[1]We should say that it is doubtful that Nebuchadnezzar is presenting himself as a god. In Mesopotamia, with few exceptions through the millennia, the kings saw themselves in a special relationship with the gods but not a god themselves.

[2]K. van der Toorn, "The Scholars at the Oriental Court: The Figure of Daniel Against Its Mesopotamian Background," in *The Book of Daniel: Composition and Reception*, ed. J. J. Collins and P. W. Flint, VTSup, 83.1 (Boston: Brill Academic Publishers, 2001), 1:37-54.

[3]P.-A. Beaulieu, "The Babylonian Background of the Motif of the Fiery Furnace in Daniel 3," *Journal of Biblical Literature* 128 (2009): 273-90.

9 DANIEL IN THE LIONS' DEN: DANIEL 6

[1]For the earlier discussion concerning the identity of Darius, see chapter 2.

[2]For the ancient Near Eastern ordeal, see T. S. Frymer-Kensky, *The Judicial Ordeal in the Ancient Near East*, 2 vols. (PhD dissertation: Yale University, 1977).

[3]T. S. Frymer-Kensky, "The Strange Case of the Suspected *Sotah* (Numbers v 11-31)," *Vetus Testamentum* 34 (1984): 11-26.

[4]Modern readers understandably have a difficult time with the idea that the wives and children of the conspirators were also thrown into the pit. It would be (too) easy to simply say that a pagan king ordered it, because it is hard to imagine that our narrator was unhappy about it. For the whole issue of violence, in particular, divine violence, see

T. Longman III, *Confronting Old Testament Controversies: Pressing Questions About Evolution, Sexuality, History, and Violence* (Grand Rapids: Baker, 2019).

10 "ONE LIKE A SON OF MAN": DANIEL 7

[1]See vol. 1 of *The Context of Scripture*, ed. William W. Hallo (Leiden: Brill, 1997–2002), 390-401 (Enuma Elish) and 241-74 (Baal Myth).

[2]See Longman, *Confronting Old Testament Controversies* (Grand Rapids: Baker, 2019), 44-48.

[3]Baal is frequently called the "rider on the clouds" in the so-called Baal Myth, for which see Hallo, ed., *Context of Scripture* 1:242-74.

[4]Specifically on pp. 41-42.

11 A RAM AND A GOAT: DANIEL 8

[1]It is ambiguous, for instance, as to whether this means 2,300 days or 1,150 days.

12 SEVENTY WEEKS: THE EXILE CONTINUES: DANIEL 9

[1]For more on the issue of the composition of the book of Jeremiah, see T. Longman III, *Jeremiah/Lamentations* (Grand Rapids: Baker, 2008), 3-6.

[2]Mark Boda, *A Severe Mercy: Sin and Its Remedy in the Old Testament* (Winona Lake: IN; Eisenbrauns, 2009), 466-68; the quotation is from 466.

13 "YET HE WILL COME TO HIS END": DANIEL 10:1–12:4

[1]T. Longman III, "Serpent," in *The Dictionary of Christianity and Science*, ed. by P. Copan et al. (Grand Rapids: Zondervan, 2017), 627-28.

[2]I am following the NIV 2011 alternate reading found in the footnote. It is true that the Masoretic Text has "sons of Israel," but since the Greek and the Dead Sea Scrolls have "sons of God," that is almost certainly the superior reading. See other translations (NRSV).

[3]For the Dynastic Prophecy and its connection to Daniel, see T. Longman III, *Fictional Akkadian Autobiography* (Winona Lake, IN: Eisenbrauns, 1991), 149-52, 187-89.

[4]S. R. Miller, *Daniel*, NAC (Nashville: Broadman, 1994), 291.

[5]Those who want to pursue more detail on this section can consult technical commentaries like J. Goldingay, *Daniel*, WBC (Nashville: Thomas Nelson, 1989) or even my more pastorally oriented commentary, T. Longman III, *Daniel*, NIVAC (Grand Rapids: Zondervan, 1999).

[6]R. J. Clifford, "History and Myth in Daniel 10-12," *Bulletin of the American Schools of Oriental Research* 220 (1975): 23-26.

PART THREE: READING DANIEL AS A TWENTY-FIRST-CENTURY CHRISTIAN

[1]H. Lindsey, *The Late Great Planet Earth* (Grand Rapids: Zondervan, 1970).

[2]H. Camping, *1994?* (Vantage Press, 1992).

[3]C. Dyer, *The Rise of Babylon* (Wheaton: Tyndale, 1991) and J. Walvoord, *Armageddon, Oil, and the Mid-East Crisis* (Grand Rapids: Zondervan), 1991.

15 HOW TO LIVE IN A TOXIC CULTURE: DANIEL 1–6

[1]D. Martyn Lloyd-Jones, *Faith on Trial: Studies in Psalm 73* (Grand Rapids: Eerdmans, 1965), 63.

[2]J. Calvin, *Daniel I (Chapters 1–6)* (Grand Rapids: Eerdmans, 1993), 76-77.

16 FINDING COMFORT IN GOD'S ULTIMATE VICTORY: DANIEL 7–12

[1]Most recently, in T. Longman III, *Confronting Old Testament Controversies* (Grand Rapids: Baker, 2019), 123-206.

[2]"Guard" is a better translation than the NIV "take care of" for the Hebrew verb *shamar*.

[3]See P. Enns, *The Bible Tells Me So: Why Defending Scripture Has Made Us Unable to Read It* (San Francisco: Harper, 2015); E. A. Seibert, *Disturbing Divine Behavior: Troubling Old Testament Images of God* (Minneapolis: Fortress Press, 2009); Gregory A. Boyd, *Crucifixion of the Warrior God: Interpreting the Old Testament's Violent Portraits of God in the Light of the Cross*, 2 volumes (Minneapolis: Fortress Press, 2017).

[4]Eugene F. Rivers III, "Powers and Principalities: King and the Holy Spirit," *Plough*, accessed November 13, 2019, www.plough.com/en/topics/justice/social-justice/powers-and-principalities.

[5]I do get into these issues in great detail in T. Longman III, *The Bible and the Ballot: Using Scripture in Political Decisions* (Grand Rapids: Eerdmans, 2020).

Author Index

Subject Index

Scripture Index

OTHER HOW TO READ BOOKS

In this series Bible scholar Tremper Longman III gives you background knowledge, literary analysis and theological input to help you read each book of Scripture as it was meant to be read.

- *How to Read Genesis*
- *How to Read Exodus*
- *How to Read Job*
- *How to Read the Psalms*
- *How to Read Proverbs*
- *How to Read Daniel*

Come discover how to read the Bible!

www.ivpress.com/academic